"HONESTLY, I COULD JUST KILL THAT CHILD!"

How many parents have found themselves muttering
such a phrase—and been shocked at their own words
about the child who means so much to them?

The sad truth is that the parent–child relationship can all
too easily turn into a destructive war of wills.

Yet raising a child need not become a series of contests
or conflicts. It can instead be a fulfilling experience that
develops a bond of warmth and understanding, nurturing
and growth—if the parent learns how to provide proper
discipline without turning into a dictator, and how to
communicate his or her wishes rather than lay down
commands.

HOWARD N. SLOANE, Ph.D., is a clinical psychologist and
professor in the Department of Educational Psychology at the
University of Utah. He is the author of numerous articles for
professional journals in psychology. Dr. Sloane is married and
the father of three children.

The Good Kid Book

How to Solve the
16 Most Common
Behavior Problems

Howard N. Sloane

RESEARCH PRESS
2612 N. MATTIS AVE. • CHAMPAIGN, IL 61821

Contents

Acknowledgments

WITHOUT the support, encouragement, and initiative of Alan Bernstein of Telesis, Ltd., this book would not exist. Nor would it exist if Judith Crandall-Sloane had not been willing to give up several months of normal living.

Gary, Jeffrey, and Wendy Sloane provided me with many years of education which contributed to this book, as well as providing specific criticism and suggestions for the chapter on communicating with adolescents.

Nancy Devenport, Janet Ward, Sigrid Kindt, and Mike Endo always responded with humor and results to my frantic cries of "rush."

Without Sid Bijou most of the procedures might not exist.

Introduction

BEING a parent is difficult. Most schools teach us little of value to prepare us to be parents, and most books provide more inspiration than help. The advice we get usually sounds good in print but doesn't work in practice. Sometimes it seems as if there is a conspiracy against giving parents any concrete, practical advice about the many problems that arise.

There is a common myth that, having been a child, a parent knows all that is needed to know about children. I don't find this very convincing. I had appendicitis once, but the experience taught me little about taking out an appendix. Though everyone will admit that children are more complicated than cars, for example, no one thinks that he can understand everything about automobiles just by observation. How can we expect to understand children, what goes wrong, and what to do about it without specific knowledge if we cannot even do this with something so relatively simple as an automobile?

This complexity sometimes prevents experts from giving parents specific advice about what to do about a problem. This is even more true when the child or the family in question is unknown. Instead, we discuss general ideas and concepts which sometimes help, but frequently fail to touch the problem. And the problem is usually very simple: Johnny is doing (or not doing) such and such—what should I do? In other words, "Help!"

In the past fifteen years psychologists and educators working from an approach called applied behavior analysis have developed some specific procedures for working with a wide range of children's problems. Several books have been published for parents which explain the general approach and principles, and they present principles of childrearing which are an excellent guide to parents who wish to develop a consistent overall approach. However, parents who have specific immediate problems and need some emergency "first aid" may find most of them too general. This book offers specific programs to help these parents. Most of the programs can be used in a variety of situations, and have been carried out by parents themselves. I have attempted to collect the practical knowledge that is so hard to find in any single source and present it in a format parents can use without professional help. I hope that practitioners will also find it useful in guiding parents. We have found that parents who are careful, serious, and concerned can carry out on their own procedures which will correct many common problems. You will find that the programs suggested correspond closely to common sense, although the steps are a bit more explicit and systematic. Few parents will have any difficulty in understanding the rationale for the programs.

These are the general assumptions of the approach used in this book:

- Most behavior of children is learned.
- The consequences, or results, of behavior usually determine whether or not a child will learn it. If these consequences are what are usually considered "pleasant" the child is more likely to learn the behavior.
- Children usually lack behavior which has not been learned. Often we assume children have learned certain things when they haven't. The solution is to teach the child what is necessary.
- What has been learned can be "unlearned" or "relearned."
- All children learn according to the same general "laws" of behavior, although they may learn slower, faster, or with more or less difficulty.
- What determines what a child will learn, or not learn, is usually less mysterious than we normally believe.

As you read, the implications of these simple assumptions will become clear.

The book is arranged so that you do not have to read the entire volume to find out what to do about a specific problem. Look in the Contents or the Index for possible chapters to consult and read these through. When you find a procedure that fits your problem you can try it without reading the rest of the book.

Success with these solutions depends upon careful reading, following the programs exactly, and using some common sense. These programs are not general philosophies; they are specific step-by-step ways to solve particular problems. Keep records where records are indicated. These records usually will tell you what to do next, whether to continue what you are doing, or whether to try something else. Without them you can't use the programs. Record keeping is usually minimal and easy.

This book does not cover the problems of parents who have infants and young babies, but it will be useful for parents of children right through adolescence. The programs are based upon the work of professional colleagues, to whom I owe a large debt. They are programs that have worked in practice, and can work for you.

1.
Because I Said So

THE Hawkins household frequently sounds like a battlefield. There is constant shouting and arguing; Mrs. Hawkins continually says "Do this" or "Do that" or "Do it now" and the children continually say "I won't" or "I don't want to" or "Do I have to?" Mr. Hawkins chimes in with "You had better do what your mother tells you or *else*," or with other threats or punishments. Despite this, things do not change—the battle goes on.

The practical requirements of everyday living require parents to give children instructions. These include self-care ("Please hang up your clothes"), chores ("Please set the table"), family relations ("Please leave your sister's book alone"), or any number of other things. Sometimes these instructions go smoothly; sometimes they do not. Instructions, of course, should not be given to a child merely to assert authority. Family life is richer, however, if children obey meaningful and reasonable instructions without argument or complaint. If you are not satisfied with the way your children follow directions, this chapter is for you.

After completion of this program, you will see a substantial increase in the number of instructions your child follows the first time you ask. And following directions will be much more pleasant for both you and your child.

Before you begin this program, please read the entire chapter.

Whom Is This Program For?

This program is designed to work best with children who have already learned to understand everyday speech but are still in elementary school. It will also work with many junior high school children. For most, this means the child is over three years of age, and under thirteen or fourteen.

Some children rarely follow parental directions. Others usually do as they are asked, but only after much argument or repetition. This program will work for both kinds of problems.

How to Begin

Read the entire program. Then explain the main points to your child, stressing that you are interested in making your interactions more pleasant. Answer any questions the child raises. Do not go into details the child does not ask about.

For a child under six years of age, make your explanation very simple, stressing the goals and the fun in achieving them.

An Honest Look: The Beginners' Program

Children frequently claim that directions given them by parents are unreasonable. Sometimes they are correct—parents can cause problems by being too demanding. Although this is not unusual or abnormal, it is wise to take an honest look at yourself before starting on the kids. Try to sit back and decide objectively if you have been trapped into making one of the three most common errors in giving directions.

Too many. Probably the most common error parents make in giving children directions is to give too many. Nobody likes to be confronted with one order after another. All of us, adults or children, need some time each day to be free from pressures.

Just how many demands is too many is tricky to determine. Neither adults nor children can escape responsibility. You will have to decide yourself if your demands are excessive. While you are relaxed, think about a typical day in your child's life. Are you always telling your child to do something? Does your child have reasonable amounts of time in which he or she does not have to worry about jobs, chores, or responsibilities? Would you feel hassled in your child's place? Go over the past two days and imagine what it would be like to be your child. Then try to come to some objective conclusion. When you feel you have a clear picture of the situation, check one of the items below:

_____ I do not feel that my child receives too many demands and directions.

_____ It is possible that my child receives too many demands and directions.

_____ It is clear that my child receives too many demands and directions each day.

If you checked either of the second two items it is important that you make fewer requests of your child each day. This means that you should go through the "beginners' program" before using the main "following directions program" in this chapter.

Too impatient. From time to time, we all get impatient. Sometimes we ask a child to do something, and before really giving the child a chance, we ask again or yell. Few people are cooperative when they receive this treatment regularly. This impatience actually prevents a child from responding properly, and deprives you of the opportunity to praise good behavior. Remember how you have interacted with your child in the past few days, and decide if you have been too impatient. Then check one of the items below.

_____ I am pretty sure I am usually not too impatient with my child.

_____ It seems likely that I am often too impatient.

_____ I know I am usually too impatient.

If you checked one of the last two items it would probably be worthwhile for you to go through the Beginners' Program before starting the main program for following directions.

Too arbitrary. It is hard for anyone to follow directions or instructions which do not make sense or which do not seem fair. It is especially hard to comply with such requests or demands in a pleasant manner. If you ask your son to brush his teeth or do his homework, this is not arbitrary; nor is a request to set the table or stop bothering somebody. But a request that merely exerts parents' authority is arbitrary. Sending a child to his or her room, for example, just because you want to be alone reading the paper in the living room is arbitrary and unreasonable. On the other hand, the same action taken because the child was screaming while you were reading might be reasonable.

Try to make an objective judgment about your demands on your child. Then check one of the items below.

_____ I usually do not make arbitrary demands.
_____ I probably make too many arbitrary demands.
_____ I definitely make too many arbitrary demands.

If you checked one of the two last items it would be best for you to go through the Beginners' Program.

— The Beginners' Program —

This program will make the main program much easier and more pleasant. The Beginners' Program may make your children more cooperative and reduce resentment and hostility, and it is likely to make you more relaxed.

The Beginners' Program is a very informal, simple program which is designed to help you see how you behave. On Day 1 of the program, record the number of directions you give your children, and indicate on how many occasions you feel you were arbitrary or impatient. On subsequent days set reasonable goals to reduce the number of directions you give, the number of arbitrary directions, or the number of times you are impatient. No definitions are given. You decide what is arbitrary, you decide when you are impatient, and you decide on your goals.

Look at the sample Beginners' Program Record. When you are actually doing the program, using the blank forms at the end of this chapter, you will write the date where we have written "SAMPLE." You will note that there are provisions to record directions given to three children. In the sample we have named the children Barbara, Alan, and Nick. For each child there are three columns to record:

A—to record Arbitrary directions.
I—to record directions given Impatiently.
O—to record all Other directions.

Now look at the columns with the numbers. These two columns are to help you keep track of how many directions you give.

For the first direction you give a child during the day, mark an X in the row by the number 1 under A if you feel the direction was arbitrary, under I if you feel the direction was followed up impatiently, and under O if neither of these was true. If the direction

BEGINNERS' PROGRAM RECORD FOR DATE OF ___SAMPLE___

Child Barbara			No.	Child Alan			No.	Child Nick		
A	1	0		A	1	0		A	1	0
		x	1	x			1			
		x	2			x	2			
x			3			x	3			
	x		4		x		4			
x	x		5	x	x		5			
		x	6			x	6			
		x	7				7			
		x	8				8			
		x	9				9			
x			10				10			
x			11				11			
	x		12				12			
x	x		13				13			
x	x		14				14			
			15				15			
			16				16			
			17				17			
			18				18			
			19				19			
			20				20			
			21				21			
			22				22			
			23				23			
			24				24			
			25				25			
6	5	6		2	2	3				
	14				6					

was both arbitrary and impatient, put an X under both A and I for number 1 for that child.

For the second direction given the same child, put a mark, or marks, under the appropriate letters opposite the number 2, in the section for that child. For further directions, orders, or requests you give the child, do the same thing opposite the correct number. Record the total directions given at the bottom, and the total for each column above that.

Starting

Day 1. Use the Beginners' Program Record for Day 1. All you do on Day 1 is record your directions, then add up and record the results. At the end of the day, look at your results. If you are trying to reduce arbitrary or impatient requests, or total requests, subtract a reasonable amount (perhaps 10%) from your scores for Day 1 and write them on the Day 2 form as a goal. If you are not trying to reduce one or more of these categories, write the same value on the Day 2 form as you scored for Day 1.

Day 2. Use the Beginners' Program Record for Day 2. Try to reduce your commands to meet your Day 2 goals. Record as usual. At the end of Day 2 add up your scores, make new goals which again are lower than the Day 2 scores, and write them as your goals for Day 3.

Days 3 and 4. On each of these days, use the record indicated for that day. Each day reduce your goal as you did for Day 2.

If you do not reach a goal. If you do not reach a goal on a certain day, do not reduce your goal for the next day. In the goal section for the next day write the same goal. If necessary, continue the program beyond Day 4, using the extra forms, until you have met your goals for three days.

When you meet your goals for three days. Go on to the next part of the program. Try to keep your requests in line with the final goal you reached.

Choosing Directions

At this point you have gone through the Beginners' Program if you felt it necessary. If you have done it successfully, you should feel that you are now reasonable about giving directions. Try to keep up your new style of giving directions. By now, or in a short time, this change should affect your child, and both of you should be more pleasant about requests. Now it is time to start the main program.

On the Directions Worksheet form at the end of this chapter, make a list of the directions you want your child to learn to follow. Include only the major ones that occur every day—do not try to cover everything. If a direction is not one that you have trouble with at least four or five times a week, omit it.

Do not list separately directions that are really variations of the same thing. For instance, "Hang up your shirt," "Hang up your jacket," and "Hang up your pants" are all merely variations of "Hang up your clothes."

You will not teach all of the directions at the same time. Try to limit the list to the fifteen most important directions. Choose those that occur most frequently, cause the most trouble, and are most important to you. Do not include directions that are arbitrary or unnecessary.

When you have completed the Directions Worksheet and, if necessary, have changed what you originally listed, be sure that:

1. You have listed at least three and not more than fifteen directions.
2. You have combined directions that are really different forms of the same request.
3. All the directions on the list are ones that cause frequent problems, are necessary, and are important.

Then go on to the next part.

Rewriting Directions

Write the first direction from the Directions Worksheet at the top of a sheet of paper. Now rephrase the direction, if necessary, so that it is in a form more likely to be followed by a child.

1. The direction should tell exactly what you want the child to do. For instance, change "Fix your room" to "Hang up your clothes, put away your toys, make your bed, and vacuum your carpet." This will make clear to both you and the child whether or not the task is complete. Some good and bad illustrations are listed on the following page.

Bad: Stop bothering your brother. Stop making him cry.

Good: Stop hitting your brother and taking his toys.

Bad: Please use good table manners.

Good: Please use your knife and fork.

Bad: Do your after-dinner chores.

Good: Please put the dishes in the sink and take the garbage to the curb.

2. Specify the time requirement, if necessary. Some directions obviously mean "right now," such as "Please use your knife and fork." Others do not make clear when the task should be completed, such as "Please put the dishes in the sink and take the garbage to the curb." A better wording might be "Please put the dishes in the sink and take the garbage to the curb by 7:15."

3. Wherever possible, reword negative instructions to make them positive. Here are some examples:

Bad: Please stop eating with your fingers.

Good: Please use your knife and fork.

Bad: Don't walk across the house in muddy shoes.

Good: Please clean or change your shoes before walking through the house.

4. Eliminate any critical remarks from your instructions. Here are some examples:

Bad: Don't be lazy; use your knife and fork.

Good: Please use your knife and fork and show us how well you can eat.

Bad: Stop being a bully and hitting your brother and taking his toys.

Good: Stop hitting your brother and taking his toys.

5. If you wish to comment on the emotional or other aspects of an instruction, stress the effect upon *you* rather than upon the child. For example, don't say "you will be nicer if you stop hitting your brother," say "I will feel happier if you will stop hitting your brother." Here are some more examples:

Bad: Please eat with your knife and fork like a grown-up.

Good: Please eat with your knife and fork so I can see how grown up you are.

Bad: Please hang up your clothes and make your bed so your room will not be a mess.

Good: I think it would be nice if your room were neat, so please hang up your clothes and make your bed.

6. With a child over age six, discuss the list to obtain the child's comments. If the child has valid objections or suggestions, take these into account and modify the list, but make sure it still meets the requirements described.

Perform these rewriting tasks for every direction where necessary on your Directions Worksheet. To make sure you have phrased every direction properly, check them against the following list:

1. Every direction tells exactly what the child is to do so that both of us can tell when it is complete.
2. Every direction that does not clearly mean "right away" specifies the time by which to complete the task.
3. Where possible, every negative direction is rephrased as positive.
4. There are no negative, judgmental remarks or criticisms in the directions.
5. Each direction that includes a comment stresses the effect upon me rather than upon the child.
6. For my child over six, each direction has been discussed with the child, and the child's comments have been taken into account.

Writing the Final Directions List

On the Directions Worksheet and the sheet of paper, you now have a list of directions that you will work with. The next step is to decide upon the order in which you will teach the directions.

Number the direction you feel the child will learn to follow most easily 1, the next easiest 2, and so forth. In determining how to do this, take into consideration the following:

1. How much trouble is it now to get the child to follow this direction? Take into account the child's comments. The easier it is now, the lower the number.
2. How complicated is the direction, and how much work does it require? A direction that a child can complete in three seconds gets a lower number, as it is more likely to be followed without argument than one requiring minutes or hours.

Write your final list on the Final Directions List at the end of this chapter, starting with the direction numbered 1 and continuing consecutively. For the moment, ignore the spaces for checking completion.

Picking and Posting
the First Three Goals

The next step is to pick the directions to start the program with, and to make clear to your child your expectations. Remove the "Our Goals" chart from the end of this chapter. Using a felt-tip pen, write the first three directions on the chart in large, clear print. Thumbtack or tape this chart in some location in your house where you and your child will see it frequently. Make sure it is at the right height for your child to see it when walking by.

Selecting Rewards

The next task is very important. It consists of selecting the rewards you will give your child if he or she meets the requirements you set up for the program. You and your child should discuss and agree upon the rewards selected. Your child will probably have many ideas that will not occur to you, many of which will be practical to use. For each section that follows, choose rewards after discussion with your child, and these should be rewards that your child would like to earn. You, of course, should suggest rewards your child might not think of, and you may have to veto some. Although several different kinds of rewards will be listed, your child will have an opportunity to earn approximately one small reward per day or one medium reward per week or one large reward less frequently.

Small rewards are privileges, activities, or items that you feel would be appropriate for your child to earn every day. For a young child, such rewards might include a story at bedtime, bedtime fifteen minutes later, an extra TV show, a special snack, or a special opportunity to play a favorite game with some family member. For an older child, privileges might also include later bedtime, school supplies, or some favorite activity or game. Select at least five such items that are acceptable both to you and to your child. Remember, the child will probably be able to earn one of these per day unless he or she would rather "save up" for a medium or large reward.

Medium rewards are privileges, activities, or items that might be satisfactory rewards for the program once a week. These might include special half-day trips or activities, a weekend movie, sleeping at a friend's house or having a friend sleep over, or some appropriate toy, hobby, sport, or school item the child wants. If a child saves for a medium reward, he will not be able to earn regular daily rewards as well. As with the small rewards; you and your child should agree upon the medium rewards selected. Pick at least three medium rewards.

Large rewards are special treats, trips, activities, or items similar to medium rewards but costly enough in time, money, or effort so that it is unreasonable to earn one per week. Try to select at least two large rewards with your child.

When you and your child have selected at least five small rewards, three medium rewards, and two large rewards, rank the rewards by yourself on a piece of paper. Put the least costly first, then the next least costly, then the next, and so on, leaving the most expensive for last. In figuring their cost, take into account actual monetary value, difficulty and inconvenience of providing the reward, and likelihood that the child will earn the reward frequently. The first, or least costly, will be the one easiest for the child to earn, while the last will be the most difficult for the child to earn.

After the rewards are ranked, remove the Reward List from the chapter and list the rewards in order on it.

Setting Up Points for Rewards

Your child will be able to earn 30 points per day for a perfect performance. Nobody is perfect, so assign a point cost of 25 to the first reward listed. Assign a point cost of 150 to an average medium reward on the list. Assign a point cost of 600 for the most costly large reward you feel the child might earn once a month if he saved most of his points for it and took few other rewards.

Using these three values as guides, assign points between 25 and 150 for rewards listed between the first reward and the one you valued at 150 points. In a similar manner, give the other rewards values between 150 and 600. It is perfectly satisfactory to have several rewards worth the same value; it is likely that several small rewards will all be worth 25. Do not worry about the exact point values. Now post the Reward List next to the Our Goals chart.

As the program progresses, you may have to change the reward values. You may do this if you find your child earning rewards too frequently or not frequently enough. Your child should get enough points to earn, on the average, at least one small reward every other day, although he or she may elect to save those for something larger. If the child is not earning this much, make the rewards cost less. You may also decide that some rewards have point values that are just too low or too high compared with other items. If you raise the cost of a reward, do it after your child has made a purchase. Announce this change a day or two in advance. A reward that is never chosen should have its value lowered.

Preparing the First Directions Card

Look at the sample Directions Card found at the end of the program. On side 1, three sample directions are written. These are the first three from a sample parent's Final Directions List. Cut out one blank Directions Card. Now look at your Final Directions List. On the card, copy directions 1, 2, and 3 from your list exactly as they appear on the list.

Look at side 2 of the sample card. Note that the names of ten days of the week have been written on the card. In the same blank spaces on your Directions Card, write in the names of the next ten days. As you will start the program tomorrow, write tomorrow's day of the week in the first spot (the top left spot corresponding to "Monday" on the sample card).

The Bank Account

Look at the Bank Account sheet found at the end of this chapter. When you start the program, write your child's name in the space provided. At the end of each day, you will write in the date, points earned, and points spent, as well as what the points were spent for. Keep track of the balance, just as you would in a checkbook.

Post the Bank Account next to the Our Goals sheet and the Reward List.

Preparing to Start

The evening before you plan to start the program, tell your child that when you both get up in the morning, you will begin. Tell him or her that he or she can get points to spend for items on the Reward List by following instructions without complaining, the first time they are given. Show your child the posted Reward List. Then show him or her the Our Goals chart, which should be posted next to the Reward List. Tell him or her that these are the directions you are going to concentrate on. Tell your child that you are sure that he or she can earn a lot of points and that you hope he or she will do well and enjoy the rewards.

How to Give and Record Directions

Starting tomorrow morning, you will begin using the Directions Card. Try to give each direction written on the card five or more times a day, unless it is the kind that you can give only once or twice. Some directions—for example, "Please empty the trash into the garbage can"—can be given only once or twice. When you give each direction, say it as it is written on the card in a normal and pleasant manner. If your child follows the direction within the time limit (if there is one), record a plus (+) in the space for that day. If your child does not follow the direction within the time limit (if there is one), record a minus (−). After a few minutes, repeat the direction, and score it again as a plus or minus. Do this until the direction is followed.

When you give a direction and it is followed correctly, praise or thank your child. Let your child know that you appreciate the cooperation. In your praise or thanks, specify frequently why you are thanking him or her. For instance, instead of just saying "Thank you," say "Thanks for using your fork and spoon the first time I asked." Do not thank the child for mere compliance by saying, for example, "Thank you for doing what you are told." The emphasis should be on what the child accomplished, not on the child's compliance. You can also stress the effect on you: "I appreciate your taking out the garbage," or "It makes me feel good to have you help by taking out the garbage."

When a direction is not followed correctly, make no comment other than eventually repeating it.

Remember to record a plus or minus for every direction given.

Figuring Out Daily Points

At the end of each day, count the total directions given from your card. This is done by adding the pluses and minuses for all three directions. For instance, on the Wednesdays recorded on the sample Directions Card, this total would be 17.

Then count the total number of directions followed. This is done by adding only the pluses for all three directions for that day. For the Wednesday sample this is 9.

To figure out the daily points, look at the Point-figuring Chart at the end of this chapter. Across the top, the numbers for "Total Directions Given" are listed. In the sample you just counted, "Total Directions" was 17; so we look in the column labeled "16, 17, 18." On the side of this chart are numbers for "Directions Followed." Nine directions were followed in the sample, so we move down the column under "16, 17, 18" until we reach the point value opposite 9. In this sample, it is 10. On Wednesday the child in the sample earned 10 points.

If the total directions given were 11 and the child followed 9 of them, how many points would the child earn? Move down the "10, 11, 12" column until you are opposite 9. What number do you find? It should be 27.

At the end of each day, therefore, you should do the following:

1. From your Directions Card, add up the total directions given.
2. From your Directions Card, add up the directions followed.
3. Look these up in the Point-figuring Chart and find the number of points earned.
4. Write the points earned in the Bank Account.
5. Write the points spent in the Bank Account.
6. Figure out the balance.
7. Tell your child how many points he or she has earned and spent and what the balance is.

Spending Points

The rewards the child earns for the points provide the motivation for the child to follow directions and to improve. It is important that you give the rewards quickly and with a positive attitude. Let your child spend points as soon as possible when he or she wants to do so. Try to give small rewards right away, preferably the same day. If the child asks for an activity or trip that cannot be given immediately or for an item that must be purchased, tell the child when you will be able to provide it. If there will be a delay of more than a day or two, give the child a Reward Certificate similar to the sample, written on a plain piece of paper and indicating when the reward will be given.

However well or poorly your child has been doing, when a reward is earned and requested, compliment the child for the work it took to earn it. Be sincere and say that you appreciate the work done to earn the reward, and stress that the child has earned the reward.

Moving Ahead

When your child has earned 24 points or more for four days in a row, it is time to move ahead. Check the three completed directions on the Final Directions List. Take down the current Our Goals chart. Make up a new Our Goals chart, and write the next three directions on it from the Final Directions List. From the same list, prepare the next Directions Card. Continue the program as before with the next three directions.

Finishing

When you have completed working on the last instruction on your Final Directions List, you are nearly ready to finish. Remove all posted materials. For about a week, give instructions from all of the Directions Cards, mixing up the order. To help you, carry all the Directions Cards with you. You do not need to record. If, in your opinion, your child does well, give him one of the small rewards at the end of the day. Praise the child each time he or she follows a direction properly. If problems arise with a particular direction, post the Our Goals chart that includes that direction. Star that direction with a crayon or felt-tip pen. Emphasize that direction, giving it several times a day. Again, give a small reward if you feel that your child did well by the end of the day.

When you have completed the program, tell your child that you are proud of how well it went. Say that you will occasionally give a surprise reward for good direction-following. At first, do this about once a week after exceptionally good days; then, less frequently as you feel inclined. As discussed, always compliment your child on good behavior.

Final Comments

In this program you learned how to gain cooperation from a child in several ways. You may have started by making your requests more reasonable. Then you reworded your requests so they were clear and unlikely to lead to an emotional reaction. Finally, you provided motivation for your child in the form of positive consequences.

THE GOOD KID BOOK

DAY 1

BEGINNERS' PROGRAM RECORD FOR DATE OF _____

Child _____			No.	Child _____			No.	Child _____		
A	1	0	No.	A	1	0	No.	A	1	0
			1				1			
			2				2			
			3				3			
			4				4			
			5				5			
			6				6			
			7				7			
			8				8			
			9				9			
			10				10			
			11				11			
			12				12			
			13				13			
			14				14			
			15				15			
			16				16			
			17				17			
			18				18			
			19				19			
			20				20			
			21				21			
			22				22			
			23				23			
			24				24			
			25				25			

DAY 2

GOALS
A = _____
I = _____
Total = _____

BEGINNERS' PROGRAM RECORD FOR DATE OF _____

Child				Child				Child		
A	1	0	No.	A	1	0	No.	A	1	0
			1				1			
			2				2			
			3				3			
			4				4			
			5				5			
			6				6			
			7				7			
			8				8			
			9				9			
			10				10			
			11				11			
			12				12			
			13				13			
			14				14			
			15				15			
			16				16			
			17				17			
			18				18			
			19				19			
			20				20			
			21				21			
			22				22			
			23				23			
			24				24			
			25				25			

DAY 3

GOALS
A = _____
I = _____
Total = _____

BEGINNERS' PROGRAM RECORD FOR DATE OF _____

Child ____			No.	Child ____			No.	Child ____		
A	1	0		A	1	0		A	1	0
			1				1			
			2				2			
			3				3			
			4				4			
			5				5			
			6				6			
			7				7			
			8				8			
			9				9			
			10				10			
			11				11			
			12				12			
			13				13			
			14				14			
			15				15			
			16				16			
			17				17			
			18				18			
			19				19			
			20				20			
			21				21			
			22				22			
			23				23			
			24				24			
			25				25			

DAY 4

BEGINNERS' PROGRAM RECORD FOR DATE OF _____

GOALS
A = _____
I = _____
Total = _____

Child _____			No.	Child _____			No.	Child _____		
A	1	0		A	1	0		A	1	0
			1				1			
			2				2			
			3				3			
			4				4			
			5				5			
			6				6			
			7				7			
			8				8			
			9				9			
			10				10			
			11				11			
			12				12			
			13				13			
			14				14			
			15				15			
			16				16			
			17				17			
			18				18			
			19				19			
			20				20			
			21				21			
			22				22			
			23				23			
			24				24			
			25				25			

THE GOOD KID BOOK

DAY 5 (If needed)

BEGINNERS' PROGRAM RECORD FOR DATE OF _____

Child _____			No.	Child _____			No.	Child _____		
A	1	0	No.	A	1	0	No.	A	1	0
			1				1			
			2				2			
			3				3			
			4				4			
			5				5			
			6				6			
			7				7			
			8				8			
			9				9			
			10				10			
			11				11			
			12				12			
			13				13			
			14				14			
			15				15			
			16				16			
			17				17			
			18				18			
			19				19			
			20				20			
			21				21			
			22				22			
			23				23			
			24				24			
			25				25			

DAY 6 (If needed)

GOALS
A = _____
I = _____
Total = _____

BEGINNERS' PROGRAM RECORD FOR DATE OF _____

Child ____			No.	Child ____			No.	Child ____		
A	1	0		A	1	0		A	1	0
			1				1			
			2				2			
			3				3			
			4				4			
			5				5			
			6				6			
			7				7			
			8				8			
			9				9			
			10				10			
			11				11			
			12				12			
			13				13			
			14				14			
			15				15			
			16				16			
			17				17			
			18				18			
			19				19			
			20				20			
			21				21			
			22				22			
			23				23			
			24				24			
			25				25			

DAY 7 (If needed)

GOALS
A =
I =
Total =

BEGINNERS' PROGRAM RECORD FOR DATE OF _____

Child			No.	Child			No.	Child		
A	1	0		A	1	0		A	1	0
			1				1			
			2				2			
			3				3			
			4				4			
			5				5			
			6				6			
			7				7			
			8				8			
			9				9			
			10				10			
			11				11			
			12				12			
			13				13			
			14				14			
			15				15			
			16				16			
			17				17			
			18				18			
			19				19			
			20				20			
			21				21			
			22				22			
			23				23			
			24				24			
			25				25			

DIRECTIONS WORKSHEET

1.

2.

3.

4.

5.

6.

7.

8.

9.

10.

11.

12.

13.

14.

15.

THE GOOD KID BOOK

FINAL DIRECTIONS LIST

_____ 1.

_____ 2.

_____ 3.

_____ 4.

_____ 5.

_____ 6.

_____ 7.

_____ 8.

_____ 9.

_____ 10.

_____ 11.

_____ 12.

_____ 13.

_____ 14.

_____ 15.

OUR GOALS

1.

2.

3.

THE GOOD KID BOOK

REWARD LIST

REWARD	POINT COST
1.	_____
2.	_____
3.	_____
4.	_____
5.	_____
6.	_____
7.	_____
8.	_____
9.	_____
10.	_____
11.	_____
12.	_____
13.	_____
14.	_____
15.	_____

SAMPLE DIRECTIONS CARD (Side 1)

1. Please brush your teeth and comb your hair right away.

2. Please take the trash from the kitchen to the curb before 7 p.m.

3. It would make me happy if you would stop calling your brother a baby.

SAMPLE (Side 2)

DIRECTIONS CARD	Mon.	Tues.	Dates Wed.	Thurs.	Fri.
No. 1	+ + + − + − − + +	+ + + + + − + +	+ + + + − − − +	+ + − + + + +	
No. 2	+ − − − − +	+ + − − +	− + + − − − +	+ − + + + + +	
No. 3	+ + −	+ + +	+ −	− + + + + +	
Direction	Sat.	Sun.	Mon.	Tues.	Wed.
No. 1					
No. 2					
No. 3					

DIRECTIONS CARD			DATES		
No. 1					
No. 2					
No. 3					
DIRECTION					
No. 1					
No. 2					
No. 3					

DIRECTIONS CARD			DATES		
No. 1					
No. 2					
No. 3					
DIRECTION					
No. 1					
No. 2					
No. 3					

```
┌─────────────────────────────┐
│ 1.                          │
│                             │
│ 2.                          │
│                             │
│ 3.                          │
│                             │
└─────────────────────────────┘
```

BACK   OF   DIRECTIONS   CARDS

```
┌─────────────────────────────┐
│ 1.                          │
│                             │
│ 2.                          │
│                             │
│ 3.                          │
│                             │
└─────────────────────────────┘
```

THE GOOD KID BOOK

BANK ACCOUNT

PROPERTY OF _____

Date	Earned	Spent	For	Balance

POINT-FIGURING CHART

TOTAL DIRECTIONS GIVEN

Directions Followed	6	7	8	9	10,11,12	13,14,15	16,17,18	19,20,21	22,23,24	25,26,27	28,29,30	31,32,33
1	5	4	4	3	3	2	2	1	1	1	1	1
2	10	8	7	6	6	4	3	2	2	2	2	2
3	15	12	10	9	9	6	4	3	3	3	3	3
4	20	16	14	12	12	8	6	4	4	4	4	4
5	25	20	18	15	15	10	8	5	5	5	5	5
6	30	25	22	18	18	12	10	6	6	6	6	6
7		30	26	22	21	14	12	7	7	7	7	7
8			30	26	24	16	14	8	8	8	8	8
9				30	27	18	16	10	9	9	9	9
10					30	21	18	12	10	10	10	10
11					30	24	20	14	11	11	11	11
12					30	27	22	16	12	12	12	12
13						30	24	18	13	13	13	13
14						30	26	20	14	14	14	14
15						30	28	22	16	15	15	15
16							30	24	18	16	16	16
17							30	26	20	17	17	17
18							30	28	22	18	18	18
19								30	24	19	19	19
20								30	26	20	20	20
21								30	28	21	21	21
22									30	24	22	22
23									30	26	23	23
24									30	28	24	24
25										30	25	25
26										30	26	26
27										30	28	27
28											30	28
29											30	29
30											30	29
31												30
32												30
33												30

SAMPLE REWARD CERTIFICATE

REWARD CERTIFICATE

This is to certify that *Teri Sherman* accumulated *300* points by *June 5th*.

To commemorate this, *a camping trip* is planned for *June 23rd*.

Congratulations!

Mrs. Susan Sherman

Parent

2.
Snacks, New Foods, and Clean Plates

MANY parents become upset when their children fail to eat what is served them at meals or refuse to try certain foods. Mealtimes become the occasion for arguing and nagging, and frequently this leads to a struggle between parents and children which neither side wins. Parents are unhappy, children are unhappy, nobody looks forward to mealtimes, and bad eating habits persist.

Although parents are rightfully concerned about the nutrition of their children, physicians say that few children suffer nutritional deficiencies because of poor eating habits. If you think your child may be suffering from a nutritional lack, you should consult a doctor. Although there is a possibility that the doctor will confirm your worry, the chances are higher that he will tell you that this is not a problem.

Some parents may worry about whether or not a child is getting an adequate diet. Others may want to be sure a child is developing healthy eating patterns which will promote health. Parents who are seriously worried about these issues would probably be wise to consult a physician. If it appears warranted, this program may help change such eating habits.

Other parents are upset over eating habits for more immediate reasons. It is difficult to plan and prepare meals if children tend to have spoiled appetites because of snacking, or to eat only a very restricted range of foods. It is also frustrating to prepare food and then have it ignored.

Unfortunately, forcing a child to eat what he doesn't want to eat usually just makes things worse. So does punishing the child for not eating. These procedures tend to make children dislike eating, mealtimes, and foods even more and result in worse eating habits than before.

Experience suggests that a reasonable, humane, and successful approach to improve the eating habits of young children cannot be based on forcing children to eat everything regardless of their preferences. However, most parents know that the preferences of young children change rapidly—that a child may dislike something today and like it tomorrow. In addition, many children develop poor eating habits at the wrong times; or they can develop prejudices about foods that they will not reconsider. Children are also often unwise in selecting what they take at the table, and in deciding how much to take.

This program is not designed to enable parents to force a child to eat everything served. It is, however, designed to do the following things:

1. To help children learn to restrict snacking before mealtime.
2. To guide children toward trying new or previously disliked foods.
3. To teach children to take reasonable portions of food so they will finish most of what is on their plates.
4. To help children restrict consumption of sweets.

Children's Diet

If you are like me, you are probably confused by the many articles written about the adequacy of children's diets. Most reasonable articles I have read suggest that healthy, normal children would benefit by following these guidelines:

1. Eating fewer foods which are mainly straight carbohydrate— that is, mostly starch or sugar. Most candies, many snack foods, soda pop, and some cold cereals fall in this category.
2. Getting more protein from fish, vegetables, and lean meats, and less from meats high in fats, such as beef and pork.
3. Using less salt at the table and in food preparation, and eating fewer salty snack foods.
4. Eating more fresh fruits and vegetables.
5. Eating less butterfat. One way to do this is to switch from whole milk to low-fat milk, and to eat less butter and similar dairy products.

6. In general, eating a well-balanced diet selected from a range of foods.

If you are concerned about this, you should consult a physician. It is sometimes difficult to determine if your children need to change their food habits, and advice from a physician can be helpful in carrying out this program. There are many published sources in books, magazines, newspapers, and government pamphlets which may also help.

How to Use This Program

First, read the entire program through from beginning to end. After you have read and understood all parts of it, come back to the snacking section, which follows, and do all the things mentioned. In a short time you should see improvement.

Snacking

The more you are able to serve meals at a consistent time, the fewer problems you will have with snacking. If on some days there is a four-hour period between lunch and dinner while on other days there is a six- or seven-hour interval, for example, you can expect to have trouble on the days with a long wait. The same is true for other meals as well. Although many people find it necessary or useful to maintain flexible meal hours, with longer waits you can expect greater tendencies to snack.

Particularly with young children, a snack may be advisable during the afternoon. Ideally, it should occur long enough before supper so it will not lead to ruined appetites, but late enough so children will not desire another snack before supper. Most parents find that a snack eaten about two hours before a meal meets these two requirements.

Preparing Snack Areas

Before you start this part of the program, you must move all snack foods that your children might eat between meals into the refrigerator or one or two selected cupboards or drawers. It is never possible to guess with complete accuracy all the things a child might eat for a snack, but using past experience, try to get all possible snack items into the two or three areas indicated.

If you are home two hours before dinner. If you will be home two hours before dinner, use this procedure.

At the back of this chapter, there is a Snack/No Snack card marked with an A. This card says "Snack" on one side and "No Snack" on the other. Two hours and fifteen minutes before you expect to actually serve dinner, hang the card by a string, with the "Snack" side showing, on the refrigerator or other obvious place. Show this sign to your children. Explain to them that when the "Snack" side is showing, it is snack time and that is the only time they may have a snack. If you typically give your children a snack, serve it while the "Snack" side is showing. If they cannot read, tell them that snack time occurs only when the smiling face is showing. Half an hour after you have hung the card up, turn it over so the "No Snack" side is showing. Explain to your children that when the card says "No Snack" (frowning face for nonreaders), they are not allowed to take a snack, but that dinner will be ready soon. Make sure they understand that if they want a snack, they must eat it during the snack time.

If you are not going to be home two hours before dinner. If you will not be home two hours before dinner, you should use the Snack/No Snack Card marked with a B. Three of these cards can be found at the end of this chapter. Note that these are divided into a "Snack" and a "No Snack" half and that each card has lines drawn at the bottom. It is assumed that at least one child will be home who can tell time.

Before you leave home, fill in the times for "Snack" and "No Snack" on the lines drawn in the lower corners. On the "Snack" side, the times should be from two hours and fifteen minutes before dinnertime to one hour and forty-five minutes before dinnertime. The time written on the "No Snack" side should be the same as the last time written on the "Snack" side.

If your children follow the snack regulations, praise them. If they do not, remove their favorite snack items from the house for two days, and in a matter-of-fact way, inform them that you have done this because they did not follow the rules. At the end of two days, return the snacks. You may have to check your refrigerator and cupboard to determine if they have followed the rules, as well as ask.

Wait until you have used the snack portion of the program successfully for four days before starting the rest of the program. Continue the snack program even after this four-day program, but combine it with the next section.

Eating Everything on the Plate

There are two secrets to getting a child to eat everything on the plate. The first is to reward success and not to punish poor eating at all. The second is to make it so easy to finish everything that kids are always successful and get rewarded. Let's see how to do this.

Making it easy. The way to make it easy is also easy: Give small portions. If you have a child who has not been finishing what is on his or her plate, you should give portions that are about a third the size of what the child has been getting. If you don't serve the child, allow only about a third of the usual serving. He or she can come back for more. The same rule holds for seconds—take (or get) only a third of the usual portion.

To motivate your child to take small portions and finish everything, announce that you are starting the "Clean Plate Club." Tell your child that he or she can earn points that can be traded in for small rewards by finishing everything and by tasting new foods or foods that he dislikes.

Look at the Clean Plate Club forms at the back of this chapter. Post one in a place your child can see after eating. Each day you should fill in the date at breakfast. For each meal, mark "yes" or "no" in the "Clean?" column. Fill in "yes" if nothing is left on the plate, including any second portions your child may have taken. Your child does not get a "yes" unless the plate is clean at the end of the meal. All other cases get a "no." Each "yes" is worth 1 point. When your child spends points for rewards, make a check in the "Spent" column for each point spent. Mark off the points earned earliest first. Because each meal marked "yes" is worth 1 point, for each point spent, put a check in the "Spent" column opposite a "yes." Thus at any time, the number of points your child has left to spend are the number of "yes" marks that have not been checked off in the "Spent" column.

Teaching improvement. Your child is now eating portions that are only a third as large as before. These are considered small portions. Stress that when the child finishes small portions, he or she may have as many additional portions of the same size or smaller, as desired. The Clean Plate Record, found at the back of this chapter, is similar to the Clean Plate Club form, only it is for your own record rather than posting, and it has slightly different information on it. Each day at breakfast, fill in the date. After each meal check the size of the portion (portions one-third as large as usual are small), and mark "yes" or "no," depending upon whether everything on the plate is finished.

After you have three days in a row with small portions that are all checked "yes," switch to medium portions. A medium portion should be about two-thirds as large as what the child typically had been taking before you started. Continue the same procedure, but mark on your record that the portions are medium.

After you have three days in a row with medium portions that are all checked "yes," switch to large portions. A large portion is merely the size portion your child normally would have. Check the "large" column and continue as before.

Rewarding good behavior. If your child finishes everything on the plate, praise the child and mark the "yes" column on the Clean Plate Club form. When you praise your child, do it in a matter-of-fact manner and do not refer to times he or she has been unsuccessful. For instance, do not say, "I'm glad you ate everything, seeing that you did so badly at lunch." Stress only the positive behavior at the current meal.

If your child does not clean his or her plate, make no comments; merely mark the "no" column on the Clean Plate Club form.

Your next problem is to decide on the rewards you and your child wish to use. With your child, look at the Reward List found at the back of this chapter. Decide with your child on four three-point rewards. These should be small rewards, such as a slightly later bedtime, a small treat, or something similar. Then pick four 12-point rewards. These should be larger rewards that might be earned only once a week, such as staying up for a special occasion, taking a short trip, or getting a small toy. Then think up four 6-point rewards of intermediate value with your child. A child can trade points for a reward whenever he or she has enough. When the child has a few points, he or she can trade them for small rewards, or he can save for large rewards. Make sure your child understands this. Post the Reward List by the Clean Plate Club Form.

Trying New or Undesired Foods

It seems reasonable that children should not have to eat foods they do not like. However, a child should taste new foods to see if he or she likes them, and the child should periodically taste previously disliked foods to see if preferences have changed.

When you start the program, the first time your child does not want to taste a new or disliked food, explain that the child will have to taste one teaspoon of the food to see if he or she likes it. Stress that you would like your child to try just one teaspoon and no more. Tell your child that a point will be awarded for tasting.

On the Tasting Record, found at the back of this chapter, write down the date, the food, and "Yes" or a "No" under "Tasted?"

When a new food is served that your child does not want to try, look on the Tasting Record. If the child has tasted that food within a week, explain that he does not have to taste the food but will get a point if he does. Fill out the chart and mark "Yes" or "No" as before. If it is a new food or a food your child has not tasted for at least a week, explain that he or she has to taste just one teaspoonful of the food.

At any time that you think it is not important, feel free to make tasting a teaspoonful optional. But do give your child the option and the opportunity to earn a point.

Again, praise your child for tasting and make no comment when the child does not taste a food.

Each "yes" on the Tasting Record is worth 1 point, just as "Yes" on the Clean Plate Club form is worth 1 point. When your child wants to spend points, you can mark them off on either record; points from both forms are equivalent. The total a child has at any time is the sum of the unspent points on both forms combined.

Sweets

You may be concerned because your children eat too many sweets. If you are, this section is for you. It covers reducing or controlling the amount of sweets taken between meals. Sweets taken as part of a meal regularly served the family (for example, desserts) are not considered in this program; reducing such sweets is part of meal planning, not a part of teaching children good eating habits as covered in this program.

Definitions. The first problem you will have to solve is to decide what foods are "sweets." As a start, try filling out the form below. Remember, for the purposes of this program anything served at a meal is not included; the child can eat whatever is served. Other than this, check the items below which apply to your situation and which you wish to restrict, and add any not mentioned in the spaces provided.

Sweet Worksheet

____ Candy bars

____ Other candy (describe) _____

_____

_____

____ Ice cream, sherbet, and other frozen similar items (sodas, sundaes, cones, dishes, malts, shakes, things on stick or cup, other as described) _____

____ Gum

____ Soda pop, except noncaloric

____ Powdered drinks or mixes which are mainly sugar (name the ones your children drink) _____

____ Sugar-coated cereal eaten as a snack

____ Cookies, cake, pie, donuts, sweet rolls, etc.

____ Plain sugar

____ Other (specify) _____

____ Other (specify) _____

____ Other (specify) _____

Be sure that:

- All sweets which you feel your child should eat less of between meals are on the list.
- You have renamed items on the worksheet where necessary, so the names are those your child knows, understands, and uses regularly for these things.
- Each item is described in a way so that your child and you will not argue over whether some specific sweet is or is not that item.

Then copy your list onto the Sweet List at the end of the chapter.

Limits. Your next problem is to decide how many treats from the Sweet List a child should have each day without any consequences. Depending upon your child, the child's health and age, and the amount of sweets the child currently eats, this will probably be between none and two. If your child is eating a lot of sweets now it will be better to be rather liberal, but to tell your child that you may reduce the amount in time. On the Sweet List you will see a space where you fill in how many sweets the child can have "free." Fill this number in on the chart.

Costs. At the end of dinner each night, have your child report how many sweets he or she has eaten since dinner the night before. For every sweet eaten above the limit allowed on the Sweet List, mark off

1 point spent on the Clean Plate Club form or the Tasting Record, the same as if a point were spent for any other reward.

If you have reason to believe that your child's report is not accurate, do not get into an argument. Casually ask if anyone else knows of sweets the child has had since dinner the night before, which the child in question may have forgotten. If anyone names another occasion of sweet eating, and the child in question does not argue, charge for that also. If there is any question, drop it.

Changing the limit. If the child was eating an excessive number of sweets before the program started, you wrote a rather liberal limit on the Sweet List. After your child has satisfactorily limited his sweets to this amount for about a week, you may wish to reduce the limit on the Sweet List. Just inform your child that you are going to do this and praise his efforts. Then cross out the old limit and write a new one—one item less. You can repeat this after every week of success until you feel the limit is a reasonable one for your child. When you reduce the limit, tell your child that as a sign of appreciation you are giving him a bonus point. Merely mark this bonus point on the Tasting Record as a "sweet bonus." After you reach what you feel is the final limit you can give your child an occasional "sweet bonus" as you see fit for maintaining a low sweet limit. Make sure you do this only at the end of a day in which your child has stayed within the limit.

Instructions, Posting, and Records

This section is a summary of the instructions you will need to give your child and the forms you will need to use. It also summarizes a few other things you must do in the program. To start the program, do the following:

1. Put all snack items into the refrigerator or in one or two cupboards or drawers.
2. Explain to the child the use of Snack/No Snack cards and use them for four successful days before going on to the rest of the program.
3. Explain to the child about the Clean Plate Club and how he or she can get a point for finishing everything on the plate. Post the Clean Plate Club form where the child can see it after meals. Fill it out after each meal.
4. Use the Clean Plate Record and decide on the size of portions the child should get.

5. Complete the Reward List, and let the child earn rewards from the list for points earned by cleaning his or her plate or by tasting. Explain this to the child and post the reward list.
6. Post and use the Sweet List, or decide it is not necessary.
7. Keep the Tasting Record, and follow the procedures that determine whether or not the child is required to taste one teaspoonful of undesired foods. Post the Tasting Record.
8. Praise success and avoid negative comments about failures.

Finishing

When you feel that your child is eating well, you may discontinue the program. I suggest that you do this in the following way.

1. Discontinue the use of Snack/No Snack cards. Tell your child that he or she still cannot snack within two hours of dinner. When this goes well for a week, go to the next step.
2. Tell your child that he or she has done so well tasting and cleaning the plate that you are going to discontinue the Clean Plate Club and the tasting procedure. If your child is younger, give him or her a filled-out copy of the Clean Plate Club Graduation Certificate found at the end of this chapter. Continue to praise proper eating and tasting and avoid making negative comments about failures.
3. Remove all posted materials.

Final Comments

This chapter has attempted to present a pleasant and simple approach to developing good eating habits. Good eating habits are in themselves important. However, good eating also plays a role in developing a pleasant family atmosphere. Mealtimes are frequently the only time when all family members get together. If mealtimes are a constant source of stress, with arguing and nagging over food, they are unlikely to be a warm time where all members of the family get together, relax, and enjoy each other. Correcting such problems is often another benefit from developing better eating habits.

snack

Snack

FROM _____   TO _____

No Snack

AFTER _____

Snack

FROM _____   TO _____

No Snack

AFTER _____

Snack

FROM _____   TO _____

No Snack

AFTER _____

CLEAN PLATE CLUB

Date	Meal	Clean?	Spent
	Breakfast		
	Lunch		
	Dinner		
	Breakfast		
	Lunch		
	Dinner		
	Breakfast		
	Lunch		
	Dinner		
	Breakfast		
	Lunch		
	Dinner		
	Breakfast		
	Lunch		
	Dinner		
	Breakfast		
	Lunch		
	Dinner		
	Breakfast		
	Lunch		
	Dinner		
	Breakfast		
	Lunch		
	Dinner		

CLEAN PLATE CLUB

Date	Meal	Clean?	Spent
	Breakfast		
	Lunch		
	Dinner		
	Breakfast		
	Lunch		
	Dinner		
	Breakfast		
	Lunch		
	Dinner		
	Breakfast		
	Lunch		
	Dinner		
	Breakfast		
	Lunch		
	Dinner		
	Breakfast		
	Lunch		
	Dinner		
	Breakfast		
	Lunch		
	Dinner		
	Breakfast		
	Lunch		
	Dinner		

CLEAN PLATE CLUB

Date	Meal	Clean?	Spent
	Breakfast		
	Lunch		
	Dinner		
	Breakfast		
	Lunch		
	Dinner		
	Breakfast		
	Lunch		
	Dinner		
	Breakfast		
	Lunch		
	Dinner		
	Breakfast		
	Lunch		
	Dinner		
	Breakfast		
	Lunch		
	Dinner		
	Breakfast		
	Lunch		
	Dinner		
	Breakfast		
	Lunch		
	Dinner		

CLEAN PLATE CLUB

Date	Meal	Clean?	Spent
	Breakfast		
	Lunch		
	Dinner		
	Breakfast		
	Lunch		
	Dinner		
	Breakfast		
	Lunch		
	Dinner		
	Breakfast		
	Lunch		
	Dinner		
	Breakfast		
	Lunch		
	Dinner		
	Breakfast		
	Lunch		
	Dinner		
	Breakfast		
	Lunch		
	Dinner		
	Breakfast		
	Lunch		
	Dinner		

CLEAN PLATE RECORD

Date	Meal	Portion (check one) Small Medium Large			Clean?
	Breakfast				
	Lunch				
	Dinner				
	Breakfast				
	Lunch				
	Dinner				
	Breakfast				
	Lunch				
	Dinner				
	Breakfast				
	Lunch				
	Dinner				
	Breakfast				
	Lunch				
	Dinner				
	Breakfast				
	Lunch				
	Dinner				
	Breakfast				
	Lunch				
	Dinner				
	Breakfast				
	Lunch				
	Dinner				

THE GOOD KID BOOK

CLEAN PLATE RECORD

Date	Meal	Portion (check one) Small Medium Large			Clean?
	Breakfast				
	Lunch				
	Dinner				
	Breakfast				
	Lunch				
	Dinner				
	Breakfast				
	Lunch				
	Dinner				
	Breakfast				
	Lunch				
	Dinner				
	Breakfast				
	Lunch				
	Dinner				
	Breakfast				
	Lunch				
	Dinner				
	Breakfast				
	Lunch				
	Dinner				
	Breakfast				
	Lunch				
	Dinner				

CLEAN PLATE RECORD

Date	Meal	Portion (check one) Small Medium Large			Clean?
	Breakfast				
	Lunch				
	Dinner				
	Breakfast				
	Lunch				
	Dinner				
	Breakfast				
	Lunch				
	Dinner				
	Breakfast				
	Lunch				
	Dinner				
	Breakfast				
	Lunch				
	Dinner				
	Breakfast				
	Lunch				
	Dinner				
	Breakfast				
	Lunch				
	Dinner				
	Breakfast				
	Lunch				
	Dinner				

THE GOOD KID BOOK

CLEAN PLATE RECORD

Date	Meal	Portion (check one)			Clean?
		Small	Medium	Large	
	Breakfast				
	Lunch				
	Dinner				
	Breakfast				
	Lunch				
	Dinner				
	Breakfast				
	Lunch				
	Dinner				
	Breakfast				
	Lunch				
	Dinner				
	Breakfast				
	Lunch				
	Dinner				
	Breakfast				
	Lunch				
	Dinner				
	Breakfast				
	Lunch				
	Dinner				
	Breakfast				
	Lunch				
	Dinner				

REWARD LIST

3 Point Rewards
   1.

   2.

   3.

   4.

6 Point Rewards
   1.

   2.

   3.

   4.

12 Point Rewards
   1.

   2.

   3.

   4.

TASTING RECORD

Date	Food	Tasted?	Spent

SWEET LIST

It will cost one point for the Clean Plate Club or Tasting Record if I eat more than _____ of the things listed below between meals. However, it will not cost anything to eat things on this list which are served as part of a meal.

1. _____

2. _____

3. _____

4. _____

5. _____

6. _____

7. _____

8. _____

9. _____

10. _____

11. _____

12. _____

13. _____

14. _____

15. _____

CLEAN PLATE CLUB
GRADUATION CERTIFICATE

This is to certify that

_____

has graduated from the CLEAN PLATE CLUB with honors,
and is entitled to all the privileges thereof.

These include taking your own portions of food
and tasting whatever you desire.

As a graduate, you will maintain the honor of the Club with Good Eating Habits.

Awarded this _____ day of _____ 19 ____ in _____

_____
Signed

3.
Not Till Your Room's Clean

"HOW many times have I asked you to clean up your room?" parents seem to say endlessly. How many times have you said or heard something to this effect?

In the larger scheme of things, problems such as a messy room may seem trivial. Problems of this sort do not affect the health or safety of family members, except in very extreme cases. But they are a part of teaching children to be responsible, and solving them can eliminate a good deal of friction between parents and children. This chapter describes an approach which will help you prevent a minor inconvenience from becoming a major issue.

Deciding What Is Reasonable

Why should a child keep a room neat? Many children say that they do not care if their room is neat, so why should others care? Then, too, how neat is neat? These are difficult questions and ones that each family must answer for itself. Here are some guidelines you might want to consider in making such decisions. Circle those that apply to your situation.

1. Is the room frequently so messy as to create a health or safety hazard?
2. Is the room frequently so messy that the child or someone else has trouble finding things?
3. Is the room frequently so messy that it is difficult to tell clean clothes from dirty ones?

4. Is the room frequently so messy that people fall or trip over things?
5. Is the room frequently so messy that it creates embarrassment when there are visitors?
6. Is the room shared with someone else who frequently is annoyed by the other person's mess?
7. Does a mess in the room occasionally result in things being broken or lost? Are equipment, toys, or games made useless because parts are missing?
8. Is the room located so that other family members cannot conveniently avoid being exposed to the mess?

If you have circled any of the above, it is probably reasonable for you to demand greater neatness. If the only reason you did not answer yes to any of the questions is that you clean the room for the child or that you continually remind the child to clean the room, then, too, it probably is reasonable for you to demand that your child keep his or her room neater.

However, parents may wish to consider the possibility that they are being unreasonable in requiring a neater room. If you answered no to the previous eight questions, consider the following.

1. Does the child have projects going that are much easier to work on if things are left out?
2. Does the child regularly clean up his room but not at the exact times that are most pleasing to you?
3. Does the child keep his room neat, but not up to your standards? If so, try to determine if it is absolutely necessary for you to impose your standards on your child.

If none of the original eight reasons for keeping a room neater applies, it is possible that you are being unnecessarily strict. Or, it may be that you have other legitimate reasons that are not on the list. Try to decide objectively, perhaps with your child, what is in fact the case.

If you have decided that the problem is with you, it would be unreasonable for you to start a program for increased room neatness. You should be congratulated for being fair and objective. If room neatness bothers you at some future time you may wish to reread this section.

Your Child's Age

From the previous section you may already know it is reasonable for you to expect your child to keep his or her room in better condition. In the following sections, we have outlined a step-by-step program to teach a child to do this. However, the appropriate standards for a clean room and exactly what jobs a child should do vary with the child's age and family. Here is a sample list of chores for a hypothetical family.

1. Hanging up or putting clothes away in a closet, dresser, or other storage area.
2. Putting away toys and personal belongings.
3. Putting dirty clothes in a hamper or other specified place.
4. Making the bed.
5. Vacuuming or sweeping the floor.

If your child is very young, you may wish to change some of these tasks or leave some out. For instance, with a young child, you may feel that you would rather decide which clothes are dirty and should be put in the hamper and which are clean and should be hung up or put away. On the other hand, you may want an older child to do additional things, such as dusting periodically. At the appropriate places in the program, add or eliminate chores to tailor the program to fit your own situation. These places will be indicated to you as you read through the program. Whether or not you add or delete items, the procedures are the same.

The Basic Rule

There is one basic rule you must follow if you want to succeed: Never clean the child's room. If you do, the child will not. If you do, the child does not have to. If you do, your child will not be rewarded for doing it or punished for not doing it. If you do, your child will never learn to clean his room.

This does not mean that you should never do anything to clean or straighten up the child's room. It simply means that you should not do the chores you assign to the child. The child must do his or her own job.

Praise Success and Ignore Failure

This is as important as the basic rule. Throughout this program, you must look for the good. Look for any positive thing your child does toward keeping his or her room clean. Look for even mediocre, half-hearted attempts. Look for any improvement. Look for the good, even if it is hard to find. When you find anything good, praise your child for it. If the room is a terrible mess but the bed is made, say, "Boy, your bed looks good." If the bed is unmade and the floor is filthy, but things are put away, say, "It looks nice to see everything put away." Praise the good; ignore the bad. The program will take care of the failures—all you need to do is carry it out.

It is important that you do this. If your child does only a part of the job, you certainly want improvement. But you do not want your child to stop doing the part, however small, that he or she has accomplished. If the bed is made and everything else is a mess, you want the child to learn to clean up the mess, but you also want him or her to continue making the bed! To ensure this, you must provide some reward for the parts that were done right; otherwise there may be no motivation to continue.

How to Start

Read the entire program through once or twice, then come back and start the actual program. In a relatively short time you will have good results.

Putting Things Away

The first step in teaching children to put things away is to make absolutely certain that they know what is expected of them. This means that they must know three things: (1) what must be put away; (2) where it should be put; and (3) by when it must be done. Again, it is not possible to give rules that will fit every family; you will have to do this to fit your own situation. Here are some samples.

- Before you eat breakfast in the morning, hang all clean pants, shirts, skirts, blouses, and jackets in the closet on hangers.
- Before you eat breakfast in the morning, put all clean socks, underwear, sweaters, and other folded clothes in the dresser.

- Before you eat breakfast in the morning, put whatever shoes you are not wearing in the closet.
- Before you eat breakfast in the morning, put all toys, games, sports equipment, and personal things on your shelves, in the closet, or in a chest.

If your children do not eat breakfast every morning, you may need to specify a time by which they are to complete their chores. You also may need a different time for Saturday and Sunday or for holidays and vacations.

In choosing a deadline for completion of these tasks, you should make sure that you will be able to check afterward to see if the jobs were done. Any time is all right, as long as you can check afterward to see that the jobs were finished and as long as there is enough time for your child to do the tasks.

At the end of this chapter is a Job Worksheet. On it, write the jobs you want your children to do. For each, make sure you specify what is to be put away, where it is to be put, and by when it is to be done. This is just a worksheet. Feel free to revise or cross out on it. Try to make your list brief—you should not need more than five items. If for some jobs you want to list a different time for Saturdays, Sundays, or holidays, do so. Now evaluate your worksheet:

- I have listed one to five jobs related to putting things away.
- For each, I have stated exactly what is to be put away.
- For each, I have stated exactly where things are to be put away.
- For each, I have stated by when a job must be done.
- For each, my child will have time to do the job by the deadline and I will be able to check to see if the job is done.

When you have met these criteria, write the jobs on the Room Chart found at the end of this chapter. Before starting the program, show the Room Chart to your child, explain it, and post it in his room.

Storage. Each day, about fifteen minutes after each job is supposed to be done, check your child's room. When you check to see if the jobs have been finished, you should collect anything listed on the Room Chart that has not been put away. For small items, take a cardboard box. Pick up everything the child has left out, as long as it is something on the Room Chart. If something that you feel should be put away is left out but it is not listed on the Room Chart, do not collect it. Talk to your child about it, and then add it to the Room Chart. From then on, if it is left out, collect it.

You should select a place to store the things you collect. A locked closet or chest is ideal. Anything put in "storage" should be labeled with a Storage Card that indicates the date it was collected and the date it is to be returned. The second date should be three days after the collection date. See the sample Storage Card at the end of this chapter. You should make up a set of Storage Cards for yourself on 3x5 cards.

You may feel that your child will not care about not having things for three days, and this may sometimes be true. But undoubtedly you will store things that your child wants to wear or use frequently enough to convince him or her to start putting things away. It isn't necessary that the child care about the loss of all things, only that some things create an inconvenience.

Bed Making and Cleaning the Floor

On the Room Chart, you will note that bed making and cleaning the floor are filled in. However, the place for you to indicate by when these jobs must be done has been left blank. Ideally, you should require that these be completed at the same time as the other jobs. However, if the other jobs are to be finished before bedtime, it may make more sense to require bed making and floor cleaning to be completed earlier. In any case, they must be done by a time that meets the following requirements:

1. They must be finished by a time that permits you to check them fifteen minutes after they are supposed to be completed.
2. They cannot be completed later in the day than the deadline for putting things away.

Obviously, it is easiest to require that all jobs be finished by the same time, and a morning deadline is preferable. On the Room Chart, fill in the times that these jobs are supposed to be finished.

In addition, in the space for cleaning the floor, different methods for completing that job have been indicated. Check "vacuum," "sweep," or "mop," or write in whatever other method you want your child to use.

You also may not want the floor done every day, or you may want it mopped on one day and vacuumed some other day. Space to indicate this is provided.

If you wish to omit either bed making or floor cleaning, just cross it out.

The procedure for reward and punishment is very simple. If the bed is not made or the floor is not clean, do not return the things from storage that day. Just cross out the date to be returned and write the next day's date.

This means that your completed checking procedure is as follows:

1. Fifteen minutes after these jobs are supposed to be completed, check to see if the floor is clean and the bed made.
2. Fifteen minutes after the deadline for putting things away, check to see that the job is done.
3. Take away things listed on the Room Chart that have not been put away, label them with the date to be returned, and put them in storage.
4. If the bed was made and the floor clean, take things out of storage that are due to be returned, and put them on the bed.
5. If the bed was not made or the floor was not clean, for the things in storage that were due to be returned today, put the next day's date on the Storage Card instead of today's, and leave them in storage for at least another day.

If the bed is not made or the floor not clean for several days in a row, keep extending the date for things to be returned from storage.

One problem that may arise is that you and your child may disagree on the standards for a clean floor or a made bed. I have found that it is best to handle this informally. If you have a problem, however, I suggest the following:

1. Be relatively lenient in your standards, especially at first.
2. The first time the bed is made very sloppily or the floor is cleaned halfheartedly, talk to your child about it. Tell your child that today only you will count this as acceptable. Point out exactly what is wrong. Tell your child that from now on it must be better, or you will not count it as done.
3. The second time the bed is made sloppily or the floor is not cleaned satisfactorily, call your child and say that it is not acceptable. Tell your child that you will give him or her five minutes to correct it this time, but that from now on it must be done correctly the first time. If it is not correct in five minutes, count it as incomplete.
4. The third time (and all other times) one of these jobs is un-

satisfactory, just treat it as if it were not done at all, without any comment.

Do not get in an argument. Just say "That's the way it is," and do not return things from storage. If your child wants to discuss the standards with you, do it at some time other than when you are checking, and go by your standards on the day in question. If, when you discuss it, your child's reasons appear sound, change the standards.

Other Jobs

Space has been provided on the Room Chart for two additional jobs. If you feel that other jobs related to room neatness should be added, we suggest that you write them on the chart and treat them just the same as bed making and floor cleaning.

Starting

If you have done the following four things you are ready to start:

1. Completed the Room Chart.
2. Selected a satisfactory storage place.
3. Prepared Storage Cards.
4. Read the entire program.

Now it is time to start.

1. Pick a time when you and your child are in a good mood to discuss and explain the program.
2. Tell your child that you want to cut down the amount of arguing you have over room cleaning.
3. Go over the reasons for having a neater room. If your child reads well, you may let him read that section of this chapter.
4. Explain that you have listed on the Room Chart the jobs you feel should be done. Show the child the chart, and explain every section of it. Ask the child if these seem reasonable. If your child has good arguments for changing any part, change that part. Do not change a part simply because your child raises a fuss, however; change it only for good reasons. Post the Room Chart in the child's room.
5. Tell your child that you will check each job a few minutes after

it is supposed to be completed. Explain that if it is not done on time, you will count it as incomplete.

6. Explain the use of storage, how you will store things, and how you will return them. Be sure to indicate what will be taken to storage, how long it will be there, and when it will be returned. Tell your child how an unmade bed or a dirty floor will prevent you from returning things that day.

7. Make sure that your child has no unanswered questions or suggestions you have not discussed about how the procedures will work. Answer all questions completely—there are no secrets.

8. Tell your child that you will start tomorrow morning.

Carrying Out the Program

You should carry out the program in a matter-of-fact but positive manner. Do not repeatedly tell your child to clean his room. Do not remind your child of his jobs. Do not criticize when the jobs are not done. And remember, do not clean the room. Simply carry out the program, letting your child take the consequences if jobs are not done. Praise success and ignore failure.

If your child never has anything in storage, but you are having trouble with the bed and the floor, you are not using the correct program. Your child basically has a neat room—there are merely a few specific chores which the child does not do. In such a case, you should look at the chapter titled "Oh, Those Chores" rather than this chapter.

To help you tell how things are going, a "Progress Sheet" has been provided at the end of this chapter. After you finish checking everything each day, fill it out. Write down the date and the number of things you had to put into storage. On days when there are many things going into storage, just write "lots." Write "yes" or "no" for the other jobs.

To reward improvement with a younger child, a Clean Room Certificate has been provided. Fill in the child's name and sign the form at the bottom. When your child has gone four days in a row with very few items put into storage and has done all other jobs, post the certificate in his room. As long as your child maintains a clean room, leave it up. When your child falls below the standards, remove it. When your child has four good days in a row again, put it up again.

Some children, particularly older ones, will not like the idea of the certificate. If your child does not wish to have it posted, you may either give it to him or omit it completely. Let your child's feelings be your guide.

More Steam

Occasionally, a child does not respond to this simple program. This is frequently because the child has so many clothes or toys that putting things in storage is not significant. If, after ten days, you see no progress you should reread the program carefully to make sure that you are doing everything correctly. If you are carrying out the program correctly, try the following:

1. Meet with your child and say that you do not feel that enough progress is being made in room cleaning. Tell your child that if he or she will try harder, you will try to make it more interesting.
2. At the back of the chapter is a "Reward List." Get this out, and with your child decide on up to five daily rewards. These should be small privileges or rewards the child can earn every day. Some examples are a slight delay of bedtime that day (fifteen or thirty minutes), a small amount of cash as a daily allowance or bonus (the amount will vary with age and family finances and philosophy), or other things you and your child might suggest and agree upon. Make sure these are all items you would not object to your child getting every day if the room is clean. Post these in the child's room.
3. Tell your child that each day the room is clean he or she will earn one of these rewards, and that you will pay the reward immediately or, if that is not possible, within twenty-four hours.
4. Tell your child that except for the rewards, everything else will remain the same.

Finishing the Program

When your child's room has been neat long enough for you to feel things are under good control (at least two weeks), do the following:

1. Remove the posted Room Chart.
2. Post the Graduation Certificate, found at the end of this chapter, in the child's room. (If your child did not want the Clean Room

Certificate posted, simply give your child the Graduation Certificate.)

3. Tell your child that you are stopping the program but will still occasionally check the room. Tell your child that as long as it looks pretty good, you will leave things this way.
4. Continue to praise success and follow the basic rule.
5. If you have been using rewards, make one of the rewards a regular privilege which your child gets every day, unless you have to remove the Graduation Certificate.

Continue this procedure unless the room starts looking messy again. If it does, tell your child that you will start the program again if he or she does not keep the room neat. If it continues to look messy, post the Room Chart again, take back the Graduation Certificate, and resume the program until things look good again.

The more you stress success and ignore failure, the less chance there is of a relapse. The less you do these things, the more likely it is that a relapse will occur.

Final Comments

I hope you found this program useful. In it you have helped your child learn to be responsible for his or her room. To do this you had to attend to several factors. The first was not to clean the child's room yourself. It is very difficult to teach a child to be responsible if the parents take the responsibility. Unfortunately, it often seems easier to do a job yourself than to try and get your child to do it. And it is easier—in the short run. However, unless you want to do everything for your child forever, sooner or later you will have to teach your son or daughter to be responsible. Therefore, if you want your child to learn to clean his or her room the first rule is to never clean it yourself. The second rule is always to accentuate the positive. This means praising the good and ignoring the failures. Although this sounds easy on paper, it is frequently difficult in practice. When a child does only a small part of a job and the rest poorly or not at all, it is only natural to get fed up. And most people are not inclined to praise the good in the face of all the bad. A more likely reaction is: "If it was so easy to clean up the toys why couldn't he have also hung up the clothes? It would have taken only a second more." Be that as it may, to get improvement we have to praise the good, and this is the second rule. Next, you must make clear exactly what is expected and what is not. Don't be vague—don't say "Get rid of that mess" when you mean "Put your clothes in the closet and your games on the shelf." In addition you must provide some simple and direct consequences for satisfactory and unsatisfactory performances by putting things in storage and, possibly, by providing rewards.

You will find that these techniques are useful in many areas of child raising. We cannot teach a child any type of chore, job, or skill if we do everything for the child. If we ignore success and attend only to our children's failures it is unlikely that they will ever have motivation to improve. I once knew some parents who never accentuated the positive. In school, if their son got an A-minus they would ask what he did wrong that prevented him from getting an A-plus. If he tried one new food they would want to know why he didn't eat other things he disliked, since it was "so easy." If he brought home a friend they really approved of they would wonder why all his friends couldn't be that nice. You can imagine the effect this sort of constant treatment had—soon the boy stopped trying to do any of the things that might have pleased his parents.

Not making expectations clear often has a similar effect. If a child is frequently told to "be good" but is never told what "being good" means, the task may seem overwhelming and impossible. Nothing is specified so maybe everything is required—perfection in a thousand vague and unclear ways. A specified goal is much more likely to be attainable and to produce results.

Finally, it seems obvious that providing some clear consequences for behavior is a good way to provide motivation. Appropriate earned rewards of this sort never lead to "spoiling" a child. However, some parents never spontaneously praise or otherwise reward their child's everyday desirable behavior. Then, if the child's behavior is unsatisfactory these parents may offer a reward (including praise) for improvement. This teaches the child to perform poorly, as rewards never occur when the child performs well as a matter of course, but only when his or her bad behavior prompts a parent to offer a reward for good behavior. A program in which consequences for good behavior are systematically planned in advance is quite different from a situation in which rewards are offered on a moment-by-moment basis following unsatisfactory performance.

JOB WORKSHEET

Job	What is to be put away	Where it is to be put	Days	Deadline for finishing the job
1			Daily	
			Saturday	
			Sunday	
			Holidays	
2			Daily	
			Saturday	
			Sunday	
			Holidays	
3			Daily	
			Saturday	
			Sunday	
			Holidays	
4			Daily	
			Saturday	
			Sunday	
			Holidays	
5			Daily	
			Saturday	
			Sunday	
			Holidays	

ROOM CHART

Job	What is to be put away	Where it is to be put	Days	Deadline for finishing the job
1			Daily	
			Saturday	
			Sunday	
			Holidays	
2			Daily	
			Saturday	
			Sunday	
			Holidays	
3			Daily	
			Saturday	
			Sunday	
			Holidays	
4			Daily	
			Saturday	
			Sunday	
			Holidays	

ROOM CHART

Job	What is to be put away	Where it is to be put	Days	Deadline for finishing the job
5			Daily	
			Saturday	
			Sunday	
			Holidays	
6	Make your bed.		Daily	
			Saturday	
			Sunday	
			Holidays	
7	Sweep ⎤ the Vacuum ⎥ floor Mop ⎦		Daily	
			Saturday	
			Sunday	
			Holidays	
8	Other (fill in)		Daily	
			Saturday	
			Sunday	
			Holidays	
9	Other (fill in)		Daily	
			Saturday	
			Sunday	
			Holidays	

SAMPLE

STORAGE CARD

Date In: _Monday, July 17_

Date to be returned: _Wednesday, July 19_

PROGRESS SHEET

Date	Approximate Number of Items to Storage	Bed Made	Floor Clean	Other

CLEAN ROOM CERTIFICATE

This is to certify that

_____

full name

has had a clean room
for 4 or more consecutive days.
It makes me very proud for

_____

to have an honor like this.

_____

Signed

GRADUATION CERTIFICATE

This is to certify that

_____

has graduated as a Room Neatness Expert
with honors
and is entitled to all the privileges thereof.
As a graduate,
you will maintain the honor of your new title
with a clean room.

It makes me feel very proud
to award you this
GRADUATION CERTIFICATE

on this _____ *day of* _____ *19* ___ *in* _____.
(city)

Signed,

_____

REWARD LIST

One of these rewards may be selected on each day for a clean room.

FIRST magnificent reward _____

SECOND marvelous reward _____

THIRD amazing reward _____

FOURTH wonderful reward _____

FIFTH tremendous reward _____

4.
No More Whining

HOW many times have parents had the following experience or one like it? You pass a child's room, and a whining, complaining voice says, "I don't wanna clean my room." Have you ever heard a whining, moaning voice say something like "Can I stay up an extra hour tonight?" If you are like most people the questions or statements themselves are not half so annoying as the tone of voice.

Young children who whine are a special kind of problem for parents. Whining is not serious; it poses no direct threat to the physical or emotional health of a child. Nor is whining alone a sign of some already existing emotional or psychological problem. Yet sometimes it becomes absolutely intolerable. Many parents do not know what to do about whining because it does not seem serious enough to warrant really strong measures. But it is so hard to put up with that the urge to do something drastic keeps recurring.

Given enough time, many children stop whining without any systematic program. But a planned approach is nearly always faster and is much more likely to produce satisfactory results than just hoping and waiting for the whining to go away.

Why whining first starts is often unclear and usually unimportant. But once it starts, it is so unpleasant that people pay attention to it or give in to the whiner just to have a little peace and quiet. The way to teach a child to stop whining is to stop rewarding the whining and to teach the child a more pleasant way of talking.

The procedures used to stop whining are fairly easy for the child, but require some changes in the parent's behavior. If you are willing to try, you should have no problem eliminating whining.

The procedures for teaching a child to stop whining are probably not worth doing unless you are sufficiently motivated. If you are, you should successfully go through the program without difficulty. If you are not it is probably just as well to merely tolerate the whining. If you frequently feel angry or annoyed at your child for whining you are probably motivated. If you occasionally refuse reasonable requests of your child because the whining way in which your child asks irritates you enough to make you unreasonable, you are probably motivated. If whining sometimes leads you to punish or hurt your child or you feel this is a possibility, you are definitely motivated.

The age of the child is also important. If he or she is very young and has little understandable speech you should not use this program. As speech develops you can then use the program if whining continues. Most children with normal speech who are between three and four years of age are old enough for this program. The program should work with children up to about age fifteen.

Although the program is simple, it is not magic. You have to be willing to carry out the steps described to be successful.

As your child stops whining he or she will be happier and easier to live with and may even get along better with other children and adults. There may be considerable results from a small amount of effort.

Check each of the following with which you feel you can agree.

_____ I have a child who whines enough to make me want to stop the whining.

_____ My whining child is at least three years old and under fifteen.

_____ I am willing to change my usual behavior with my child in order to teach the child not to whine.

If you were able to check all three, this program is for you.

The Approach

A child will never learn to stop whining if whining is the only way to be heard. Sometimes parents get so busy or so used to a child's whining that they never pay attention to the child unless the child whines. It is very important that throughout this program, you always pay attention to anything your child says in a nonwhining tone of voice. Children learn to whine because whining frequently works better than speaking in a normal tone of voice. The reason whining works is that it is unpleasant; people pay attention to it or give in so the whining will stop. The cure is to reverse things—to make pleasant tones of voice pay off more than whining.

If your child talks to you at a moment when you do not have time to listen, take a brief moment to make some temporary answer like "That sounds interesting, but I am really in a rush now. Could you tell me about it in a few minutes when I can really listen?" Better yet, if at all possible, take time to listen to your child right away. Listening to your child when he or she speaks normally will motivate him to continue to talk this way.

Most children whose habit of whining is really annoying whine in many situations, particularly those in which they want something. This program is designed mainly for this problem. A few children, however, whine only when they are asked to do something. If this is your situation, read the entire program. After Step 5 in the program, you will find special instructions for handling this more specific type of whining.

In Step 1 you do four things. You explain to your child why whining bothers you. You demonstrate to your child a better way to talk. You then have your child perform in this better way. Finally, you reward your child for talking more nicely.

Obviously, you want your child to learn to perform these skills spontaneously and independently. So after several days of the four-part program (Step 1), move to Step 2. Step 2 is the same as Step 1 except you omit the demonstration—by now your child already knows what is expected. Step 3 goes even further toward making your child independent of help from you; both the explanation and the demonstration are omitted. Step 4 polishes this by encouraging the child to use a pleasant tone of voice from the start, while the final step covers how to prevent whining from recurring.

How to Start

Before doing anything about whining, read the entire program. The program has a practice exercise for you to do with another adult or with an older child who is cooperative and does not whine before you start working with your whiner. Read through the program and do the practice exercise. Then go back to the beginning and start the actual program with your child.

It is unlikely that your child whines only with you. There are probably other people in the family who are annoyed by whining and who might be interested in decreasing it. This may include other adults or older brothers and sisters. If they are interested they may go through the whining program with you. However, if brothers and sisters are included they should be quite a bit older than the child in question, old enough so they do not tease or boss.

If several people are going to try the program together there are several rules to be followed. These are:

1. Everyone should read the program and discuss it together before starting.
2. Copies of the practice sheets and summary sheets should be made for each individual.
3. Everyone should do the practice exercise. It is fine if those involved in the program do this with each other.
4. In carrying out the actual program, everyone must carry out the steps exactly as they are written.
5. In carrying out the program, everyone should be doing the same step on the same day.
6. Everyone carrying out the program should meet for five minutes each evening to discuss how it is going and to make sure that everyone is doing the same thing.

A carefully carried out group program will be more effective than if one person does the program while others continue to act as they have in the past.

Step 1: Explaining, Demonstrating, and Rewarding Performance

If your child has been whining for some time, a habit of whining has probably been well established. The first step is to make sure that your child knows more acceptable ways of talking. To teach these, you are going to have to do four things:

1. Explain to your child each time he or she whines that talking in a whining voice is very unpleasant to you.
2. Demonstrate a better way to say what the child is trying to get across.
3. Ask your child to say what he or she wants in this better way, and have your child perform it.
4. Reward your child for a better performance.

It cannot be stressed enough that your success will depend on your carrying out this exact procedure (described in more detail in the following material) every time your child whines. After several days, you will switch to a simpler procedure. Here are the four steps, explained in detail.

Explaining. We all find it easier to comply with other people's requests if we understand the reasons for them. Unexplained demands often sound arbitrary, and may frequently provoke antagonism rather than cooperation. To help get your child's cooperation you should simply and honestly tell him or her that whining makes you feel bad. Telling a child how you feel is perfectly legitimate and a reasonable basis on which to request a change. Which of the following two statements would you predict is more likely to gain cooperation rather than antagonism?

- "Please stop that right away!"
- "That really makes me upset—please stop it right away!"

Most people would probably react more favorably to the second. The brief explanation makes the demand sound much more reasonable.

When your child starts to whine, stop him and make a brief statement that meets the following requirements:

1. The statement must not criticize the child, or say anything negative about the child.
2. The statement should stress how whining makes you feel, as long as it does not criticize the child. Some good examples are:
   - "Whining makes me feel bad."
   - "When I hear whining it makes me feel that I don't want to listen."
   - "I get upset when I hear whining."

Below are some statements a parent might make when a child starts to whine. Using the two guides and the examples above, check each as OK or NOT OK. If you check a statement as NOT OK, indicate why. Then check your answers with the printed answers.

1. "Whenever I hear whining it makes me feel bad."
   OK   NOT OK
   (This statement is OK, as it merely states how you feel.)
2. "When you whine, I feel that you are a baby."
   OK   NOT OK
   (This statement is not OK, as it makes a critical remark about the child.)

3. "I just don't like talking like that."
   OK   NOT OK
   (This statement is OK, as it merely states how you feel.)
4. "Whining makes me want to go out of the room."
   OK   NOT OK
   (This statement is OK.)
5. "Whining is what spoiled brats do. I don't like it."
   OK   NOT OK
   (This statement is not OK, as it makes a critical remark about the child.)

When you are sure about all of these statements, write three statements below that you might make when your child whines. Then check them against requirements 1 and 2.

1. _____
   _____
   _____
2. _____
   _____
   _____
3. _____
   _____
   _____

Remember that all statements should be brief, preferably just one sentence.

Demonstrating. In this beginning stage you wish to make sure that your child is absolutely certain of the correct way to speak. After you have explained to your child how whining makes you feel, demonstrate a better way to talk. There are two aspects to this: the particular words said, and the tone of voice. You will have to imagine the correct tone of voice. For example:

Child: "Aww, Mommy, can't I have just one little cookie now, huuh, please, can't I?" (Said in a crying, whining voice.)
Parent: "When I hear whining, it makes me feel like not listening. Try saying it like this: 'Mom, may I please have a cookie now?' "

Performing. Your goal is not to have your child stop talking to you, but to have him or her learn to talk in a more pleasant manner. So you must let the child practice a more appropriate way of talking.

After your child hears you demonstrate the correct way to talk, he or she will probably say it correctly. If your child does not spontaneously speak again, say, "Say it the way I did." If your child does say it correctly and in a reasonable tone of voice, go on to rewarding, described in the following section. To be rewarded your child does not have to say exactly what you did, but merely has to repeat the original idea without whining.

If your child does not respond at all or whines again, tell him or her once again to try to say it properly. If the child does not respond or continues to whine, ignore your child completely until he or she says it correctly. This is the hardest part. After you have given your child one more chance you must act as if you cannot even hear a whining or crying child. Do not act annoyed or angry, but do not respond to the whining. If you pay attention to whining now you will have taught your child the wrong thing—what he or she may learn is that if whining does not pay off the first time, whine, whine again!

If your child eventually repeats the original or a similar statement in a pleasant manner, you should reward it, as described in the next section.

For new whining on a new topic start the procedure over, with an explanation.

Rewarding. If your child talks to you in the correct way after the explanation and demonstration you should reward him. This will increase the chances that your child will continue to talk in a more pleasant manner, although this is unlikely to occur after just one successful attempt. A reward can be granting a request or a simple "thank you." If you can grant a request, do so. If you cannot, tell your child you wish you could, why you cannot, or when you can. In any case, thank your child for talking so nicely. Say things like:

- "I like the way you said that."
- "It makes me feel good when you talk like that."
- "Thanks for asking like that."

Any time your child requests something from you or talks to you without whining, provide a reward and thanks.

Practice. The procedures for Step 1 are summarized on the Step 1 Summary Sheet found at the end of this chapter. In order to practice Step 1, you need help from another adult or an older child who does not whine. Read the Step 1 Practice Sheet found at the back of the program and explain it to your helper. Then go through the Step 1

Practice Sheet. You should use the summary sheet; your helper should hold the practice sheet. Each person who is going to use the program with your child should do the practice exercise.

Carry it out. When you have read the entire chapter and done the practice, start Step 1 with your child. If more than one adult is going to do this, all should start and end a step on the same day. Do Step 1 for *four* days. Then go on to Step 2.

Step 2: Skip the Demonstration

When your child asks you for something without whining, reward the child as you did in Step 1. When your child whines, explain how you feel about whining, as you did in Step 1, and ask your child to repeat correctly what he or she has to say. In Step 2, however, you do not demonstrate the correct way of saying it. By now your child should have a good idea of what is expected, and you do not want to make your child dependent upon repeated demonstrations.

For example, if a child has just whined, you might say, "It makes me feel bad when you whine. Please say it correctly."

If the child responds correctly, give a reward. If the child whines again or makes no response, say once, "Please say it properly." If your child does, give a reward. If the child does not say it correctly, ignore the child.

If the child corrects himself or herself, or says it or something else correctly a little later, give the reward.

As you can see, this is very much like Step 1, only without the demonstration. The procedures are summarized in the Step 2 Summary Sheet found at the back of this program.

Carry it out. After you have finished Step 1 with your child for four days, do Step 2 for four days. Then go on to Step 3.

Step 3: Ignoring Whining

By now, your child should certainly be able to respond correctly without whining, although he or she may not do so every time. In addition, the previous steps may have made your child somewhat dependent on your reminders or guidance to speak correctly. Step 3 is designed to get more consistent and independent results.

When your child whines. By now you should be hearing only occasional whining. Now you have to get tough. For many people, this is the most difficult part of the program. When your child whines, ignore it completely. Do not talk to your child, no matter how long he or she keeps whining. Do not attend to the child physically by holding, cuddling, hitting, or anything else. If possible, do not even look at your child. If you find it difficult to refrain from all these things, get up and walk away or go to another room.

It is very important that you stick to this procedure. If you start to ignore your child but then pay attention after some whining has occurred, all your child will learn is that the way to get attention is to whine louder and longer. Hang in there—it will not be for long.

When your child does not whine. When your child speaks to you without whining, tell the child you like it when he or she talks to you this way. If you can, grant the request. If you cannot, tell your child why not or when you will be able to do so. Do this even if the child first spoke to you in a whining voice and then said it properly. In any case, respond pleasantly with approval.

These procedures are summarized in the Step 3 Summary Sheet found at the back of the program.

Carry it out. After you have completed Step 2, carry out Step 3 for four days. Then go to Step 4.

Step 4: Rewarding Appropriate Talk Only When It Occurs the First Time

By this point you should be hearing very little whining and lots of appropriate tones of voice. However, some children may have learned to whine first and then to correct themselves, or to make a quick correction after seeing what you do. This step is very much like Step 3, with one exception. Again, if your child whines, ignore him or her. However, after your child has asked you something in a whining voice and repeats it in less than three minutes, you should say, "If you had asked me without whining the first time, I could have listened to you. Ask me again in three minutes." If your child asks again in three minutes without whining, reward. If he or she asks before three minutes are up, just say, "Wait till your three minutes are up." If the child still whines, ignore the child. If the child asks you correctly the first time, or at least three minutes after whining, reward.

The goal of this step is to help your child learn to talk without whining the first time. Continue this step for two days. Read the Step 4 Summary Sheet at the back of this chapter.

Carry it out. After you completed Step 3 go to Step 4 for two days. Then go to Step 5.

Step 5: Final Procedure

This is the final step in the program. It is often wise to continue it indefinitely. It is similar to Step 4, except that you do not give any sort of reminders or instructions to repeat what was said. If your child whines, ignore the child. Also ignore the child if he or she repeats the same request in a reasonable tone of voice within three minutes of whining. Each time your child whines you should start timing the three minutes over again, so the child can never get a response from you within three minutes of the last whining statement. If your child speaks reasonably or repeats something reasonably at least three minutes after whining, reward and praise the child. The Step 5 Summary Sheet is found at the back of this chapter.

If Your Child Whines Only When Asked to Do Something

Some children whine only after being asked to do something by a parent or adult, not when requesting something from an adult or in ordinary conversation. But if you ask that the garbage be taken out, that the child get ready for school, clean his or her room, or set the table, you hear, "Annhh, do I have to do it now?"

The way to handle this depends upon whether after whining the child does what is requested anyway. Many children seem compelled to make some whining remark after a request even though they comply with the request. If this is the problem you have, the solution is simple: Just ignore the whining completely from the beginning. Do not respond to it in any way either with words, gestures, or facial expression. However, praise the actual performance of the requested task. This will usually get rid of such whining without any other procedures.

If you have problems actually getting your child to do his or her chores or to follow directions, you should read the chapter which covers your specific problem and follow those procedures. You may also ignore whining as described above.

Final Comments

One of the amazing things about children is how much more easily they often seem to learn unpleasant behavior than pleasant behavior. In following this program you probably noticed how parents teach things to children. If whining receives attention from a parent a child is likely to learn how to whine; this is even more true if the child is often ignored when speaking in a more pleasant manner. Here, you tried to turn this around, so the child got more attention for appropriate talk than for whining. In addition, explanations and examples were used to speed up this new learning. I hope you were successful in solving this trivial but annoying behavior problem and that both you and your child now find life more enjoyable. It is likely that you will find the general principles and techniques useful in a variety of situations.

STEP 1 PRACTICE SHEET

INSTRUCTIONS. Pretend you are a child asking a parent for something. Do each of the following exercises three times, but mix up the order. Each time you do one, check it off in the space provided. When all spaces are checked three times, practice is finished.

____ Ask for something nicely, without whining.

____ Ask for something by whining. When you are corrected, do not respond.

____ Ask for something by whining. When you are corrected, whine again.

____ Ask for something by whining. When you are corrected, respond as instructed.

____ Ask for something by whining. When you are corrected, do not respond. After ten seconds, respond correctly.

____ Ask for something by whining. When you are corrected, whine again. After ten seconds, respond correctly.

____ Ask for something by whining. When you are corrected, whine again. After ten seconds, whine again.

____ Ask for something by whining. When you are corrected, whine again. Then remain silent.

____ Ask for something by whining. When you are corrected, whine again. After ten seconds, continue to whine and whine.

STEP 1 SUMMARY SHEET

IF YOUR CHILD ASKS FOR SOMETHING WITHOUT WHINING—REWARD
A. If possible, grant the request.
B. If it is not possible to grant the request, tell your child why not or when you can grant the request.
C. Thank the child for asking nicely.

IF YOUR CHILD WHINES
D. Without being critical, explain in one sentence how whining makes you feel.
E. Demonstrate a better way to say it.
F. Ask the child to perform correctly if this has not already happened.
G. If the child responds properly, go to parts A, B, and C above.
H. If the child does not respond at all or whines again, tell the child once more to say it properly.
I. If the child then responds properly, go to parts A, B, and C.
J. If the child again does not respond or whines, ignore the child.
K. If the child says it properly, go to parts A, B, and C.

CONTINUE FOR FOUR DAYS.

STEP 2 SUMMARY SHEET

IF YOUR CHILD ASKS FOR SOMETHING WITHOUT WHINING—REWARD
A. If possible, grant the request.
B. If it is not possible to grant the request, tell your child why not or when you can grant the request.
C. Thank the child for asking nicely.

IF YOUR CHILD WHINES
D. Without being critical, explain in one sentence how whining makes you feel.
E. Ask the child to say it properly, unless this has already occurred.
F. If the child responds properly, go to parts A, B, and C above.
G. If the child does not respond at all or whines again, tell him once more to say it properly.
H. If the child then responds properly, go to parts A, B, and C.

I. If the child again does not respond or whines again, ignore him.

J. If the child finally says it properly, go to parts A, B, and C.

CONTINUE FOR FOUR DAYS.

STEP 3 SUMMARY SHEET

IF YOUR CHILD ASKS FOR SOMETHING WITHOUT WHINING—REWARD

A. If possible, grant the request even it the child whined initially.

B. If it is not possible to grant the request, tell your child why not or when you can grant the request.

C. Thank the child for asking nicely.

IF YOUR CHILD WHINES

D. Ignore your child completely.

E. If your child finally says it properly, go to parts A, B, and C above.

CONTINUE FOR FOUR DAYS.

STEP 4 SUMMARY SHEET

IF YOUR CHILD ASKS FOR SOMETHING WITHOUT WHINING—REWARD

A. If possible, grant the request.

B. If it is not possible to grant the request, tell your child why not or when you can grant the request.

C. Thank the child for asking nicely.

IF YOUR CHILD WHINES

D. Ignore your child.

E. If your child repeats within three minutes something he or she has whined about, say, "If you had spoken to me without whining the first time, I could have listened. Ask me again in three minutes.

F. If your child then speaks properly but in less than three minutes, say, "Wait till your three minutes are up."

G. If your child still whines, ignore him or her.

H. If your child asks or speaks again after at least three minutes without whining, go to parts A, B, and C above.

CONTINUE FOR TWO DAYS.

THE GOOD KID BOOK
STEP 5 SUMMARY SHEET

IF YOUR CHILD ASKS FOR SOMETHING WITHOUT WHINING
   A. If possible, grant the request.
   B. If it is not possible to grant the request, tell your child why not or when you can grant the request.
   C. Thank the child for asking nicely.

IF YOUR CHILD WHINES
   D. Ignore your child.
   E. If your child repeats something he or she has whined about in less than three minutes, ignore the child.
   F. If your child asks again after three minutes without whining, go to parts A, B, and C above.

CONTINUE INDEFINITELY.

5.
Stop That Fighting, Arguing, and Teasing!

MOST children fight, tease, or argue at times—some frequently, some on only rare occasions. So do most adults. Children fight over nearly anything—who can have a toy, who said what, who did what, whose turn it is to do something. As we all know, fighting, yelling, shouting, arguing, name calling, teasing, and being mean to one another are not unusual.

Not unusual, but certainly unpleasant. Sometimes fighting gets out of hand and becomes more than unpleasant. Although some adults seem to have a great tolerance for squabbling, many find that it gets on their nerves. Children often seem to enjoy fighting and arguing, but when it gets out of control they usually change their minds quickly. In any case, most adults find that children are happier in the long run in an environment with minimal fighting and arguing

There are many reasons that children fight or tease. Most of these reasons are just what your common sense tells you. One reason is that it works. The successful fighter gets the toy or the first chance to try a game. The aggressive child usually is able to get other children to play his or her way or to do what he or she wants. This is especially true in situations where it is not clear who has a right to certain things. If it is clear that the toy robot belongs to Marty, there is less likelihood of fighting. If it is definitely Amy's turn to use the telephone, arguing is less likely than when it could be Amy or Marsha's turn. Even when fighting is merely meaningless teasing or name calling, it may occur because it works; it helps establish a pecking order so the child established as a leader can get his or her way.

Fighting and teasing also get a lot of attention. You may have observed that one main result of squabbling is that it is noticed. Other children, as well as adults, pay attention to it. Attention is a powerful reward at most ages.

Children also fight in imitation of other children, adults, TV, movies, or books. Sometimes this starts out as play. You have probably seen young children start to act out a somewhat violent TV show and end up getting into a serious fight. If parents fight, children may imitate them. Children are very poor at learning to "Do as I say, not as I do." If a child sees that other members of the family solve problems by fighting, or that TV or movie heroes do so, we can expect the child to try the same techniques.

Parents often reward children for being aggressive without realizing they are doing so. Many parents want their male children to be "manly," but if a parent rewards a child for taking physical action against another, this may encourage fighting in general. Alternate ways of "standing up for yourself" might be considered.

Finally, there is evidence to suggest that the more a child is punished the more the child will fight. This may even happen when a child is punished for fighting itself! However, in this case the child may learn to fight when no adults are looking.

Most fighting, squabbling, and arguing does not indicate some serious psychological problem. It occurs for reasons which are fairly obvious and uncomplicated once we think about them. Most parents who are willing to make a serious and consistent attempt to get rid of fighting can do so, and can develop a more pleasant, relaxed, and healthy atmosphere in their homes.

Before you start, read the entire chapter and make sure you understand all aspects of it.

Whom Is This For?

The program in this chapter is designed to work most effectively with children between the ages of five and twelve. It will, however, also work with children as young as three and with many children older than twelve. The program suggests several different options; you must decide which is best for your child.

The intelligence of the children involved is not a critical problem. The program should be effective with bright, average, and slower children. Obviously, the program may go more quickly or slowly with some children than with others, but the procedures described do not depend upon intelligence.

Similarly, it will work as well for children with a variety of handicaps as for those without such problems. The child's speech level is not important; many things described can be modified so that language is not required.

The program is not designed to handle all types of aggressive problems. Serious aggressive behavior that is dangerous to others requires professional help and procedures that work faster than those described in this program. Group or gang aggressive behavior, for example, is a problem requiring other procedures. This program is mainly for reducing ordinary squabbling among children, regardless of why the fighting or arguing developed.

How to Begin

Read and familiarize yourself with the entire chapter and all the materials. After you are sure about exactly what you are going to do, the program will tell you how to explain this briefly to the children involved.

The program has six major parts. The first helps you decide exactly what your problem is. The second is aimed at reducing fighting and arguing by helping you eliminate one of its causes. The third part helps you rearrange situations at home that lead to fighting and arguing. The fourth part suggests consequences for fighting and arguing that should make them less frequent. The fifth part tells you how to decrease situations in which children may learn to imitate fighting, arguing, or teasing. A final part tells you how to reward good behavior so that fighting, arguing, and teasing become less frequent. You may decide to use all of these procedures, or just those that fit your problems best.

What's Your Problem?

Most people think they know the answer to this question, but they often turn out to be not so sure when they try to state it clearly. Try to list your problems, step by step. Descriptions of some common problems will be presented, and all you have to do is check them off if they apply to your situation. Space has also been left for you to write in individual types of fighting, arguing, and teasing that are not included in the list. In filling in this "diagnosis" of fighting and arguing, there are two rules you must follow:

1. List only important and frequent problems—the major ones that cause most of the problems.
2. State exactly what a child does or says. Do not list what he or she "tries" to do or what a child "intends" to do or "wants" to do. Here are some examples of good and bad statements:

   Bad: Tries to get the other child angry.

   Good: Bumps into the other child or slides his things off the table onto the floor.

   Bad: Makes the other child feel inferior.

   Good: Tells the other child she is stupid or ugly or incompetent.

   Bad: Picks on the other child. Picks on brothers and sisters.

   Good: Disagrees with and contradicts everything brothers and sisters say.

Make sure that the differences between the "good" and "bad" statements above are clear to you. The bad case in the first example describes what the child "tries" to do. From this it is not possible to tell what the child actually does. One person might decide that when a child ignores another the first is "trying" to get the other angry. Another might disagree and say the child is "trying" to avoid a fight. As the statement does not tell what the child actually does it is unclear. The good example in this case describes what actually happens and is much easier to agree upon. The second example requires you to be a mind reader, to determine whether or not a child "feels inferior" as a result of what another child has done. In addition, it does not describe the behavior; it merely lists its effects. The final bad example leads you right into the middle of children's arguments and teasing. No one can ever agree on whether one person is "picking on" another, and using a definition of this sort will just lead to further fights and arguments. The good example states clearly what the child does.

Below is a list of types of fighting a child might do that are actual physical attacks of some kind. Check each one that is an important part of your problem. In the spaces at the end, fill in and check any other physical attacks that apply to the situation with which you are concerned.

_____ 1. Hits, kicks, bites, bumps, punches, slaps, bends arm of, throws down, or elbows the other child or children.

_____ 2. Throws things at another child or children, drops things on other children or does one of the things in No. 1

using an object, such as bumping another child with a chair or book.

____ 3. _____
_____
_____

____ 4. _____
_____
_____

____ 5. _____
_____
_____

Below is a list of types of fighting and arguing a child might do that are directed against the things of another child. Check each one that is an important part of your problem. In the spaces at the end, check and fill in any others that might apply to your situation.

____ 6. Breaks or throws things.

____ 7. Moves or hides things. Takes things without permission.

____ 8. Takes things away from another child.

____ 9. _____
_____
_____

____ 10. _____
_____
_____

____ 11. _____
_____
_____

Here is a list of things a child might say in teasing, fighting, or arguing. Check the ones that apply. Check and fill in others that apply to your particular situation.

____ 12. Calls another, or the work or things of another, derogatory or insulting names.

____ 13. Threatens another.

____ 14. Comments negatively on another's behavior.

____ 15. States that bad things will happen to another.

____ 16. States that another child did something the other child denies, or states that another child did not do something the other child claims to have done.

____ 17. _____
_____
_____

____ 18. _____
_____
_____

____ 19. _____
_____
_____

Perhaps there are some types of fighting, teasing, and arguing in your situation that do not fit any of the categories. If so, list them below.

____ 20. _____
_____
_____

____ 21. _____
_____
_____

____ 22. _____
_____
_____

____ 23. _____
_____
_____

Go over all the items you checked and make sure that every item is important, occurs frequently, and states exactly what a child does or says.

The Work List

On the Work List at the end of this chapter, summarize the important types of behavior you have just listed. Go over the items you have listed on the preceding pages. Rewrite them, in order, on the Work List. Study the Work List until you have a clear idea of exactly what types of behavior are the problem.

Reducing Punishment

It may surprise you to read that the next step in getting rid of fighting, teasing, and arguing involves reducing the amount of punishment you give your children. There are two reasons for this:

1. The more discipline your children are currently receiving, the less your new program will stand out as something new and different and the less effective it will be.
2. As stated, evidence suggests that the more children are punished, the more they fight and argue.

If you want to reduce fighting, teasing, and arguing, it will pay to reduce punishment as much as possible. The trick is to do this without adversely affecting other behavior.

To start, we must mention that parents are human. When they are tired, irritated, in a bad mood, worried, or overworked, they frequently tend to be grouchy with their children. This may take the form of critical remarks, a short temper, more strictness, or greater punishments. These kinds of remarks or actions, whether they are the result of a child's behavior or a parent's mood, may lead to later increases in fighting and teasing.

Think carefully about the past two days. You can probably think of some instances when you were critical or punished your child too severely or without good cause. In the spaces provided, try to list some examples of this that have occurred in the past two days.

Example 1: _____

Example 2: _____

Example 3: _____

Example 4: _____

Example 5: _____

Example 6: _____

Example 7: _____

Example 8: _____

_____

The first step in this program, then, is to reduce the amount of unnecessary punishment or criticism. It would also be good to increase positive remarks and praise when children are behaving well. To help you do this, fill out the Positive/Negative Sheet at the end of this chapter. When you start the program, fill it out each day. Each day try to increase the number of positive remarks and decrease the number of negative remarks.

Avoiding Fighting and Arguing

There are a number of situations that commonly lead to fighting or arguing. The next step in our program is to identify these situations and try to change them.

You may be surprised as you do this section to learn how much trouble comes from a small number of specific situations. It is extremely difficult to recognize the situations that lead to fighting, teasing, or arguing when you are in the middle of them. These are much more likely to become clear when you sit back for a moment and complete this part of your program.

Competition. There are several types of competition that arise frequently and are related to fighting or arguing. These are:

1. Competition over a toy, book, sports equipment, TV, telephone, personal belongings, etc.
2. Competition over who goes first. This often overlaps with type 1 above; children may argue or fight over who can use something first.
3. Competition for attention. Children sometimes fight and argue to get attention. Often this attention is from an adult.

Undoubtedly, you can think of other types of competition that occur in your own home.

Disagreement. Fighting and arguing often occur over disagreements. Common disagreements involve:

1. Whether a person said or did something to another.
2. Whose turn it is to do a certain task.
3. Who owns or has something—"Is that my record?" "Do you have my comb?"

Nearly everybody could add things to this list, but these suggestions will start you thinking about possibilities. Fill out the "Common Situations" column of the Fighting and Arguing Situations form at the end of this chapter, by describing the situations that lead to fighting. Add to it or correct it by observing your children for the next three days.

Now that you have information on the situations that often precede fighting and arguing, here are some suggestions for using this information.

Records. Some fighting and arguing situations can be reduced by keeping written records that resolve the issue in question without fighting or arguing. Here are some examples of types of situations where records can help.

1. Whose turn it is to take out the garbage.
2. Whether or not a child borrowed someone else's belongings.
3. Whose turn it is to use the phone.

A paper with a space for date and name can be posted in a conspicuous spot to record who last performed a chore. When a person takes out the garbage, for example, have him sign the list, put in the date, and record the time the task was performed. The basic rule is simple: If a person forgets to sign the sheet, it is the same as if that person did not do the job. Such a list for chores can avoid much arguing and fighting. The same procedure can be used for taking turns. If children argue over who gets to choose the television show, a record can be made showing whose turn is next. If any of the situations that you have recorded in the first column of the Fighting and Arguing Situations form are the type that a record will help, write "Record" in the second column. Then make such a record on a plain piece of paper. When the record is posted, explain it to your children. When it is in use, check the "In Use" column on the form.

Labeling. Many arguments over who owns what can be resolved by labeling items. Each item that is argued over regularly should be labeled, and so should each new item that becomes a cause of fighting. If you have situations of this sort listed in the first column, write "Label" in the second column. When the item is labeled, explain the process to your children. Check "In Use" when the labeling is completed and has been explained.

Timing. Fighting or arguing over the use of the telephone, a phonograph record, or similar things can often be avoided by imposing a time limit. For instance, telephone calls can be limited to ten minutes, after which it is somebody else's turn. Put a timer by the telephone, and post the rule. Similar use of a timer may reduce other arguments. If this fits any of your situations, write "Timing" in the second column, and explain the rule to your children. When you are using the procedure, check off "In Use."

Other. There are many ways that fighting and arguing can be avoided, and different situations call for different approaches. If there are items in the first column of your list for which records, labeling, or timing will not work, you might think of an approach of your own. If you do, describe it in the second column and check it off when it is in use.

If none of the ways to avoid fighting and arguing fit some of your situations, do not be discouraged. For those situations that nothing fits, leave the second and third columns blank. When the form is complete, go on to the next part.

Providing Consequences for Fighting and Arguing

Although punishment and certain situations contribute to fighting and arguing, the major factors that cause fighting and arguing to continue are the rewards they provide. The most common rewards for fighting and arguing are:

- Attention from adults.
- Attention from other children.
- The payoff. This may include one child getting his or her way with another, getting a toy, or stopping another child from doing something. Or it may involve an adult letting a child do something or letting a child avoid something.

It is usually difficult, without great expense in time and effort, to determine precisely which consequences are important for a particular child. The procedures that follow cover all of the possibilities.

Minor teasing, fighting, and arguing. If fighting and arguing are about a toy, a possession, or an object, take the object when the squabbling starts. Tell the children that when one of them can come up to you and quietly and politely tell you who they have decided is to get the object, you will return it. If the arguing is over the use of something, announce that none of them can use it until one of them comes up to you and quietly and politely tells you who is going to use it first. If arguing occurs over something already in use, make them stop using it, and do the same thing. Other than doing these things, ignore the children completely (unless the teasing or arguing becomes more serious, in which case follow the next procedure). If the minor teasing, arguing, and fighting is over nothing in particular, as long as it stays minor, just ignore it completely.

More serious teasing, arguing, and fighting. When teasing, arguing, and fighting become more serious, different tactics are needed. Serious means it is physical, or so loud that it disrupts or interferes with the activity or conversation of others. Act the minute you see such arguing and fighting—do not wait even a second. If it is clear to you that a particular child started the scene, use the procedure for that child only. If it is not entirely clear who is at fault, use the procedure for everybody involved. The procedure is simple: Send everybody involved to their rooms for ten minutes. If some of the children share the same room, pick separate rooms to send them to; which room is not important. Do this every time serious fighting and arguing occurs.

To make sure you understand what is to be done, here are some sample situations. After you read each one, describe what should be done. Also note whether timing, records, or labeling could have been used.

1. Frank, seven, and Joe, nine, are building something. They are using family tools. Joe yells, "My turn to use the screwdriver." Frank says he is not through. Joe yells louder, stating that Frank has had it for ten minutes. Frank says that's not true, that Joe just had it for ten minutes. Both get louder and louder until they can be heard all over the house.

What to do: _____

_____

_____

2. Mary, eleven, yells at Brenda, thirteen, and says that Brenda has her hairbrush. Brenda says that it is her hairbrush—the brown one is Mary's. Mary says that is a lie. Brenda tells her she is wrong and that it is "tough." Mary screams that Brenda is a pig, picks up the brush, and throws it at Brenda.

What to do: _____

_____

3. Allan, ten, and Sara, twelve, are downstairs. Allan is on the phone. Sara screams that he has been on too long and she has to call her friend. Allan says he just got on. Sara says he has been on the phone for thirty minutes. Both start grabbing for the phone and shoving each other.

What to do: _____

_____

_____

4. Terry, four, and Carla, six, are building something out of piled boxes. Terry whines at Carla and says, "You moved my box." Carla says Terry moved her box. Terry whines some more. Carla tells Terry that she is a baby. Terry tells Carla that she "stinks." They both build as they argue.

What to do: _____

_____

_____

5. After dinner, Sam, thirteen, tells Frieda, ten, that it is her turn to clear the table. Frieda says it is his turn. Sam insists it is her turn. This argument continues for ten minutes.

What to do: _____

_____

_____

6. Don, nine, and Ron, eight, both want to use the bicycle. They squabble over who had it longest, whose turn it is, and they shout and cry in the yard.

What to do: _____

_____

_____

7. Alice, thirteen, tells Brian, eleven, that he is a creep, and Brian kicks her in the leg as hard as he can. Whatever led up to this is not known.

What to do: _____

_____

_____

Here are my answers. If you did not agree with them, go over this section again until it is clear to you why I selected the courses of action I did. You still may not agree with all.

1. Send both to their rooms for ten minutes (they are being very disruptive). Then keep the screwdriver until they can ask you for it politely and tell you who will use it first.
2. Send Mary to her room for ten minutes (she is being very disruptive). Label the brushes.
3. Send each to his room for ten minutes (they are being very disruptive). Then do not let either use the phone until they can tell you politely who will use it first and for how long. Use timing.
4. Ignore them. This is only minor squabbling over nothing in particular.
5. Post a record to avoid future problems.
6. Take the bicycle until they can tell you quietly who will use it first and for how long. You might use a record if this is frequent.
7. Send Brian to his room for ten minutes (he is using physical violence).

Look at the sample Procedures Form found at the end of this chapter. It has room for ten sample situations. To fill out this form, merely observe your children when fighting and arguing starts. Do not do anything about the fighting. In the sample spaces write down what happened and what you would have done if you had started the program.

Reducing Models Children May Imitate

We noted that one factor which can increase children's fighting, arguing, and teasing is imitation of people who engage in this behavior. These models may be from real life, TV, movies, or books. It is often difficult to determine if this is a problem, and sometimes even more difficult to correct. Go through this section and try to make a judgment; then make those changes which seem reasonable. To help you do this, in the back of the chapter there is an Imitation form.

Adult models. If children see adults in their family fight, argue, or tease they are more likely to do so. Sit down with the adults in your family and discuss this problem. Explain that you are trying to determine if your child's or children's fighting, arguing, or teasing may be in imitation of adults who do this. Tell everybody that you do not want to get into a discussion or argument over who in the family fights or who is in the right or the wrong. The purpose of the discussion is solely to help the child or children.

Ask each person if he or she has engaged in a fight or argument at home within the week. Tell everyone you do not care what it was about, just whether it occurred. After all have given their opinions, have all make a judgment as to whether this is occurring so frequently that a child might imitate it. If it is frequent, list the situations in which fighting and arguing occur on the Imitation Form and indicate who is usually involved.

Once you have decided that this may be a problem, the next step is to determine what to do about it. The best solution is to get all to agree that they will not fight or argue when children are present. Try to get such agreement. Adults should also agree to two further things: (1) to remind one another if children are present when a fighting, teasing, or arguing situation is beginning, and (2) to fight, argue, or tease in some private place where they will not be overheard by children. For those who agree, mark on the Imitation form under "What to Do" that they will go to some private place. Have the people involved initial this to remind them of their commitment. For those who do not agree there is probably little you can do, so ignore it and mark "nothing" on the form.

Peer models. Some children may have friends or others they spend time with who engage in a lot of teasing, arguing, and fighting. On the Imitation form mark the situations in which this occurs (at home, playing after school, etc.) and the friend or persons involved. Then determine if there is any way you can reduce the time your child spends with these persons. Here are some suggestions on how to do this. Select the ones which seem appropriate for the situation, and for the relationship you have with your child.

1. Discourage or forbid your child from being with that person or going to that situation. Do this only if you can do it easily and without causing a scene. If your child objects violently, drop this.
2. Encourage your child to spend time with other people than the fighter, arguer, or teaser, or actually invite others over.
3. Find activities that your child will enjoy at the times the child usually is with this friend.
4. Forbid such other children in your house unless they can act in a better manner. If they do come in and engage in teasing,

arguing, or fighting, tell them you are sorry, but they must go home. Tell them that they can come back another time if they will behave properly. Be matter-of-fact and do not make an issue of it. By telling them that they can come back another time you will probably get less of an emotional outburst from your child or from the friends.

Fill out the section on "peers" on the Imitation form showing what you have decided to do.

TV, movies, and books. If your child engages in aggressive behavior and watches TV or movies or reads books where violent behavior is depicted you should try to reduce such activities. On the Imitation form list under "Who or What" the violent TV shows, movies, or books your child regularly watches or reads. Under "Situation" indicate when this occurs. There are several things you can do, but only do those which will not create a big ruckus. Some possibilities are:

1. Forbid or discourage your child from watching that show, going to those movies, or reading those books.
2. Encourage alternate shows, movies, or books which are not violent.
3. Encourage alternate activities at the times these things occur.

In some households it may be very difficult to do much about changing existing aggressive models. Do not make a big issue of it. Do those things which you feel are important, and let the others go. Your goal is to reduce these models for aggressive behavior as much as you can without creating a whole new set of problems. Do the best you can, and leave it at that. When you have finished, complete the sections of the Imitation Form.

Starting

At this point you should be familiar with nearly all the major procedures of the program. Now you have to explain the program to your children, decide (with them) on some positive rewards that will be given for cooperation and success, and figure out some simple way to keep track of how things are going.

1. Explain the program. Tell your children that you are starting a program to make life more pleasant for all of you by having less fighting and arguing. Tell them that the program will probably

have many parts to it that they like, and a few that they do not like. Your children may claim that they do not fight or argue excessively. If they do, tell them that however much or little they fight or argue, it has gotten to the point where you want to reduce it. Tell them that you are quite sure that they will have more fun once they do. Do not tell them that what they have been doing is "bad" or "naughty" or "immature" or anything else negative.

2. Show and post the Work List. Show your children the Work List and tell them that these are the main types of behavior that have been bothering you. Read each item on the list, and explain it to them. If they argue, ignore it and go on. Merely say, "These things bother me, even if you do not think they are problems." Then post the Work List on the wall where all the children can see it daily.

3. Explain any use you are going to make of records, timing, labeling, or other similar procedures. Make sure that records are posted in an appropriate place, that labels are on, and that timers are close to where they will be needed, such as by the telephone. If you have any notices you have made to go with this, make sure they are posted. Tell your children that from now on these procedures will be used.

4. Explain about consequences. Explain when a child will have to go to a room for ten minutes. Explain when you will remove items and make them unavailable. Answer any questions. Tell your children that, starting now, these procedures are in effect.

5. Explain what you are doing to avoid imitation of bad examples. If you have decided that your children may get involved in teasing, fighting, or arguing because of bad examples from adults, friends, TV, movies, or books you should briefly explain this to them. There are various ways you can express this, such as:
   - "I think some of the grown-ups have been fighting a lot and setting a bad example for you," or
   - "It seems to me that some of your friends do a lot of arguing and may encourage you to do the same," or
   - "I'm concerned that some of the TV shows you watch tend to give the idea that fighting, arguing, teasing, or violence are a good way to act."

When you do say these things to your children, avoid any criticism of the children or the people involved. Look at the first example which was just given. Notice that it does not criticize anyone—for instance, it doesn't say, "Your father and older brother don't know how to act and are always getting into fights." Look at the second example and you will see it does not directly state any negative opinions about the children's friends or about the children themselves. For instance, it doesn't say, "Your friend George is a bad influence and has no manners; all he does is shout and fight," nor does it say, "Some of the people you pick for friends show what terrible judgment and standards you have." Avoid any negative statements of this sort and just stick to the facts—this is likely to cut down the amount of argument you get from your children.

After you have briefly explained what concerns you, you should tell your children what you would like to do about it. Do this in an open and pleasant way. Say "I'd like to see if things will improve if we cut out watching *Blood and Guts* on TV every Saturday night for a few weeks," rather than "I've decided that you cannot watch *Blood and Guts* anymore."

If you get a negative reaction to your explanation you should compromise rather than get into a fight. For instance, you might suggest trying some suggestions and dropping others. Then as the program proceeds you can decide whether adding the rest is critical. In any case, do not insist on your children avoiding TV shows, movies, books, or friends if it appears this will create more problems than it solves.

Good Behavior Contract

Everybody finds it easier to change his or her behavior if there are rewards for changing. In the long run the reward is, of course, a happier home atmosphere. However, some more concrete and immediate rewards in the beginning will help quite a bit. The Good Behavior Contract and the rewards associated with it are designed to provide these rewards in an effective and uncomplicated manner.

Look at the Good Behavior Contract at the back of this chapter. Count the number of children signing the contract. Write that number in the two spaces marked with an asterisk.

Go over the contract with your children. Tell them that it is designed to help them get rewards for days on which they do not engage in any of the types of behavior on the Work List or engage in only a very few of them. Read the entire contract through with them. Fill in the blanks. Sign it and date it. Explain that for each day none of the children performs even one of the types of behavior on the Work List, each child will get 2 points. Explain that if all of the children combined perform fewer than the number listed in the spaces with asterisks on the contract each child will get 1 point. Explain that on any day during which more than this number occur no one will get any points. It will not matter if one child performs several of the types of behavior or if each performs one; only the total number performed by all children on the contract counts. All children get the same number of points each day. Post the Contract by the Work List.

The rewards. Look at the Reward List at the back of this chapter. With your children, decide on two to four 1-point rewards. These should be small rewards, such as a slightly later bedtime, a small treat, or something similar. Then pick two to four 10-point rewards. These should be larger rewards that might be earned only once a week, such as staying up for a special occasion, taking a short trip, getting a small toy, etc. Then, think up two to four 2-point and 5-point rewards of intermediate value. Children can use points for a reward whenever they have enough points. When they have only a few points they can spend them for small rewards or they can save for large rewards. Make sure all the children understand this. Post the Reward List by the Work List.

The point record. Each child should have a Point Record. Give each child a copy of the Point Record, found at the end of this chapter, and have each put his or her name at the top. Fill out the Point Record each day, and keep track of the balance, just as you would the balance in a checkbook.

Here is an example to make sure this is clear.

Date	Earned Today	New Balance	Spent	For	Final Balance
11/3	2	2	1	TV	1
11/4	1	2	0	—	2

Make sure that each child understands the procedure. Tell them that whenever they spend points, you will enter it on the Point Record. Post the Point Records by the Work List.

How to Keep Track

Keep the blank Procedures Form handy. Each day, if any types of fighting or arguing behavior on the Work List occurs, write them on the Procedures Form. At the end of the day, using the Procedures Form, write the points on each child's Point Record. You do not have to keep track of each individual child's behavior, since the contract is a group contract.

Finishing

When you feel the fighting and arguing are at a reasonable level, you are ready to end the program. I suggest that you keep the consequences in effect and do not discontinue them and that you do the same with records, timing, and labeling. You may, however, drop those that you feel are no longer necessary.

Remove all the posted materials, and tell your children that you are discontinuing the contract. Tell them that occasionally, when they have been good, you will give them a treat. Praise them frequently when they have been good and have not fought or argued for a while, making sure they know that you appreciate it. Once in a while, when things have been going very well, have a special treat. Make sure that your children know that it is because they have acted well and that there has been little fighting, teasing, or arguing.

In this chapter you have learned how to use a variety of procedures to reduce fighting, teasing, and arguing. First you pinpointed the actual types of behavior which are problems. You also learned to reduce punishment and bad examples which children might imitate. You set up procedures to avoid situations which lead to disagreements. Finally, you established consistent positive consequences for good behavior and some negative consequences for bad behavior. If you systematically follow these procedures you should see a substantial improvement over time. How fast this will occur will depend upon a number of things, but you probably will not see any appreciable results in less than four days and should certainly see some major improvements within two weeks.

Learning to handle negative behavior of children is frequently very difficult. This chapter should help you deal with these difficulties without feeling that your own behavior is worse than your children's. If you carefully set up your program and then carry it out in a relaxed, matter-of-fact, and systematic way, you will get results.

THE WORK LIST

1.

2.

3.

4.

5.

6.

7.

8.

9.

10.

11.

12.

13.

14.

15.

16.

17.

18.

19.

20.

21.

22.

23.

24.

Each day, write a " + " mark in the POSITIVES column for each positive remark made to your child(ren), and a " − " mark in the NEGATIVES column for each punishment or negative remark. At the end of each day, count the marks and fill in the totals.

DATE	POSITIVES	NEGATIVES	TOTAL POSITIVES	TOTAL NEGATIVES

FIGHTING AND ARGUING SITUATIONS

Common Situations	Ways to Avoid	In Use

PROCEDURES Check Each Item That Should Have Been Used

Describe What Happened	Records	Labeling	Timing	Other (describe)	Ignore	To Room	Remove Object

THE GOOD KID BOOK

PROCEDURES   Check Each Item That Was Used

Describe What Happened	Records	Labeling	Timing	Other (Describe)	Ignore	To Room	Remove Object

PROCEDURES   Check Each Item That Was Used

Describe What Happened	Records	Labeling	Timing	Other (Describe)	Ignore	To Room	Remove Object

IMITATION

Type	Who or What	Situation(s)	What to Do
Adults			
Peers			
TV			
Movies			
Books			

GOOD BEHAVIOR CONTRACT

This contract is entered into in an effort to promote more pleasant surroundings with less fighting and arguing.

In exchange for less fighting and arguing, I_____

Parent or Guardian

referred to as the parent, agree to reward_____

List each child involved

_____

for days in which no fighting or arguing occurs.

On any and every day during which *none* of the behaviors listed on the WORK LIST occurs, each child signing this contract will earn two (2) points.

On any and every day during which no more than ____ * of the behaviors listed on the WORK LIST occur, each child signing this contract will earn one (1) point.

On any day during which more than _____* of the behaviors listed on the WORK LIST occur, no points will be earned.

These points may be exchanged for the rewards listed on the REWARD LIST.

Signed this ____ day of _____ , 19___, in _____

_____   _____
         Parent   *Child*

                                 _____
                                           Child

* See page 114.   _____
                                           Child

POINT RECORD

Name_____

DATE	EARNED TODAY	NEW BALANCE	SPENT	FOR	FINAL BALANCE

POINT RECORD

Name_____

DATE	EARNED TODAY	NEW BALANCE	SPENT	FOR	FINAL BALANCE

THE GOOD KID BOOK

POINT RECORD

Name_____

DATE	EARNED TODAY	NEW BALANCE	SPENT	FOR	FINAL BALANCE

REWARD LIST

Rewards worth one point

1.

2.

3.

4.

Rewards worth two points

1.

2.

3.

4.

Rewards worth five points

1.

2.

3.

4.

Rewards worth ten points

1.

2.

3.

4.

6.
Helping with Homework

DO Your Homework . . . do your homework . . . do your homework! Familiar? It is to thousands of children and parents. In some families it is a regular evening scene, scheduled like one of the TV shows. The kids don't like it, the parents don't like it, and it doesn't work, but it keeps occurring night after night.

It is obvious that for most children getting homework done on time is essential, but many students plan to study more than they actually do study. Sometimes they just don't get around to it. Other things come up and get in the way. Sometimes they begin and stop before completing the task. Boredom or distraction may set in. If you have a child who often ends up not doing as much homework as seems reasonable, this program is for you.

Why is it so hard for most children to do homework regularly? No single answer will fit every individual. A major reason is that doing homework usually competes with more desired activities. Most elementary and high school children actually have only about three hours of free time a day! If you do not believe this, look at the schedule below for one typical young child.

Sleeping . . . . 8 hours
In school . . . . 6 hours
Travel to and from school. . . . . ½ hour
Breakfast, dinner, plus preparation and cleanup. . . . . . 1½ hours
Washing, dressing, bathroom . . . . 1 hour
Home chores . . . . 1½ hours
Shopping, doctor, dentist, errands, other trips
    with parent . . . . 1½ hours

Homework .... 1 hour

Free time .... 3 hours

TOTAL .... 24 hours

As you can see, children have a busier life with less free time than most adults think. So homework really competes significantly with a child's leisure.

In addition, many children find homework boring. Much homework is not new, interesting material, but is drill or practice on skills already learned. For children who have not learned the skills the homework requires, the task is especially difficult. Unfortunately, an occasional teacher assigns busy-work—that is, work designed merely to take up time. This occurs when a teacher feels children should have homework, but does not have anything of significance prepared. Finally, consequences for homework are often very remote or completely lacking. Some teachers do not collect homework regularly, or do collect it but do not grade it, or grade it but hand it back to students after a long delay. Some teachers never make clear to children why the homework is important, and how it will count in their school program or grades.

However, even when homework is meaningful and important to the school program, children often have difficulty developing the work habits to do their assignments in a regular manner. This is not surprising when you realize that most of us have never been taught how to work regularly on our own. This is a skill which must be learned, and here is your chance to teach it to your child. After completion of this program, you will be able to help a child to do homework alone, steadily, and regularly for a reasonable length of time. You will know how to get a student to *spend time studying*.

How to Begin

Read the entire program. Then explain all of it to your child. If he or she has further questions about how it operates at a later time, answer the questions. But do this only if asked.

Find a Place

Your child must have a place to study. It doesn't have to be fancy and it doesn't have to be a separate room. Ideally, of course, study space should make it convenient to study. Read each of the requirements for study space below and record the location on the Study Guide at the end of the chapter.

1. *Physical requirements:* adequate light; a place to write; a comfortable businesslike chair; supplies such as pencils, pencil sharpener, glue, erasers, and ruler nearby so that the student does not have to leave the study location.
2. *Privacy requirements:* screened from sight of other locations or people or activities (of course, a separate room does this, but it is not necessary) and shielded from sounds of other activities. If the study is *not* a separate room, the student should not face the rest of the room. A large screen may be useful.
3. *Use of study space:* The study space should never be entered except to study. When a student is not studying (even for a three-minute break), he or she should not be in the study area. When a student is studying (at home), it should be in the study area. Spaces that may be used for other activities (play, listening to music, entertaining friends, writing letters, talking on the telephone, eating, etc.) are not good.
4. *Lack of distractions:* There should be no telephones, TV sets, record players, food, pictures, books, or magazines unrelated to current homework assignments, or other distractions in the study area.

Decide on a Time Schedule

Now that you have prepared a space, you must decide when it will be used. There are three elements to a time schedule: what time of day your child will study, what days your child will study, and how long your child will study. Before you begin the program, figure these out and write them on the Study Guide at the end of this chapter. Plan this with your child.

1. *How long to study.* Find the average daily time the student *now* spends doing homework over a five-day period. This will be the beginning length of his or her study period. Write the number of minutes in the Study Guide. Even if it is only fifteen minutes, that will be the beginning time. If it is less than ten minutes, begin with a ten-minute period.
2. *What time.* Before starting the program, decide upon the time at which the student will start doing homework. If possible, this should be at the same time each day.

3. *What days.* Decide upon which days of the week the student will normally do homework. With efficient studying, most students find five days a week will usually do the trick.

Rate the Student

At the end of each study period you are to give the child a rating on studying. There are three possible ratings, described in the chart.

Rating	Meaning
Success	The student works for the entire homework period. No attention is paid to whether assignments are completed or done correctly. If the student spent the required amount of time in the study location, and you did not definitely see him or her engaging in activity other than study, the student's word is the basis for judging whether or not he or she worked during the homework period.
Failure	This means that the student went to the study location, but did not work for the entire homework period.
No game	This means that the student did not go to the study area. This may be because the student had no homework, did the homework elsewhere, or did not do the homework at all. In all cases, it is rated "no game."

The ratings should be given immediately after the termination of the study period.

When to Change the Length of the Homework Period

Decide on what you consider the ideal length of the homework period for the child's age, grade, and school. Consult the child and the child's teachers if necessary. Write the goal below.

Ideal length of homework period:____
Write the student's beginning length of homework period here:____

Increase the length of the period five minutes when the student gets five success ratings in a row with no failure ratings. Ignore the "no game" days. Keep doing this until the homework period reaches the ideal length.

Until you feel that the program is no longer necessary, do not allow the child to work longer than the homework period. If the child wishes to finish something after the homework period has expired, he or she may, but not in the study area. Work done outside this area is not considered "homework" for the purposes of this program. The reason for this is simple. If a child has an extra amount to do or works very slowly on a certain day, he or she may continue working until even the idea of homework becomes disagreeable. You do not want this unpleasantnesss to become associated with the homework area. In addition, with extra work the child may have to stop before the assignment is completed. You want the homework area to be associated with success, not failure.

Keep a Chart

Keep a chart as a record of the success the child has each day in completing the homework period. On the chart, mark both the length of the homework period required for that day, and the actual time the student did homework in the study area. A sample, and space for continuing, is provided on the following page.

A nine-day sample is provided. Note that the current required homework period is marked with a dotted horizontal line. In the sample, for all nine days it was fifteen minutes. The actual homework time for the student is shown with solid dots for each day, connected by a solid line. In the sample, on the first day the student studied fifteen minutes, meeting the requirement, as he also did on the second, fourth, fifth, seventh, and ninth days. On the third day he studied twelve minutes. However, on the sixth day he did not study at all. On the eighth day he studied for thirteen minutes, two minutes short of the requirement. There were six "successes" out of nine days!

In the extra space provided, or on a separate graph, keep your own record showing the daily homework period required as well as the actual study time.

Provide Motivation for Success

What to use. With a young student, a special but small privilege or treat should be given for "success." At the start of each week, this should be decided on in conference with the student. It may be a special trip for five or more "successes." It may be being allowed some

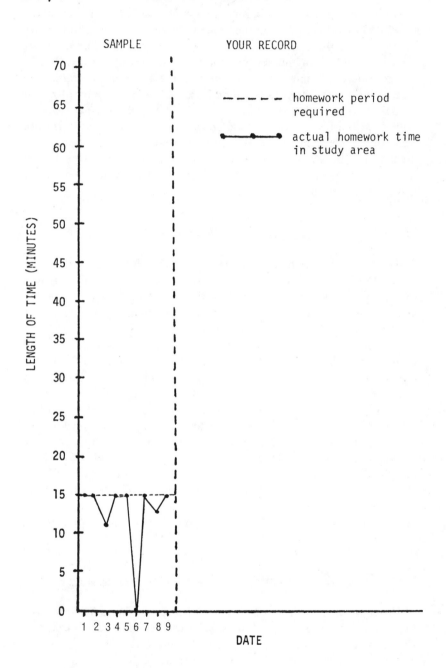

other privilege. The parent and the child are the best judges of what is appropriate.

With an older student with poor homework habits, also select as a reward some highly preferred activity or time. A good way to tell what is a highly preferred activity is by the frequency with which the individual does it. Typical rewards used by parents are watching TV, listening to a record player, using the family auto, going out with friends at night, allowance, the privilege of following some fad, and so forth.

List some possible privileges or treats which might be used. Do this in conference with the child.

1. _____
2. _____
3. _____
4. _____
5. _____
6. _____
7. _____

How much? The biggest problem is to determine how much of the privilege is earned by each day of "success" in doing homework. The guiding rule is as follows: Each success should be worth enough so that if the student succeeds every day, he or she will receive more of the privilege than before the program, but each success should have a low enough value so that if the student shows no improvement, he or she will receive less of the privilege than before the program. How to do this will be explained.

Here is an illustration. One boy, whose program started with a ten-minute homework period, liked to watch TV all the time. His parents estimated that in recent weeks they had allowed him to watch TV about an hour a day. They also estimated that in recent weeks he had done at least ten minutes of homework less than half the time. By making each success worth two hours of TV, he would have to be successful at least half of the time to watch as much TV as he watched before the study program started; that is, one hour per day. However, if he always did his homework, he would be allowed to watch two hours per day, or twice as much as before the study program started.

Some rewards may require several successes to earn. For instance, a parent may decide that each time a child earns five successes, he or she can go to a movie. Others may be small, so that even one success may earn some reward.

Let the child spend the rewards as he or she wants—that is, allow the child to save them up for the future or to spend them daily. Do not give any reward if the child does not score a success. Do not use anything as a reward unless you are willing to let the child get even more of it than he or she is currently getting, since the value of each success should be such that as the student does the homework every day, he or she will get more of the reward than before.

Encourage the older student to suggest possible motivators to you, and to let you know if he or she would prefer a new one. If one seems to lose its appeal, change to a different reward. However, do not change if the student does not wish to do so, as long as he or she is regularly earning successes.

With young students, when you first start the program and for at least eight days thereafter it is best to have a privilege or treat which they can earn daily. This is also best with older students in the very beginning of the program.

If you feel up to it, you can allow the student to trade in successes for a variety of rewards. For example, you might make each success worth a hundred minutes of TV or thirty-five cents allowance. If you do this, give the student the option of spending his successes as he desires.

List below how many successes each of the rewards you listed previously cost—that is, how many successes are required for a reward, or how much reward each success earns.

1. _____
2 _____
3. _____
4. _____
5. _____
6. _____
7. _____

Preparing the Records

At the end of this chapter is the Reward Table. Write down on this table the rewards you and your child decided upon and listed earlier in this chapter. Where necessary, include "how much" of the reward is included. In the space provided also list the number of successes required to earn each reward.

At the end of this chapter there is also a Success Sheet. This sheet should be filled out just before the child goes to bed every evening. One row is for each day. Each night, put the day before's "New Balance" in the column marked "Prior Balance." For the first day only, merely put a zero in this space. Then, if the child earned a success on the day in question, put a 1 in the "New" column. If the child spent any successes that day, put the number of successes spent under "Spent." It is useful to know which rewards the child spent successes for, so make a brief note indicating the reward in the "For" column. This information may help you if you wish to add or drop any rewards, or raise or lower any of the costs. Finally, add any new successes to the day's prior balance, subtract any successes spent, and write in the new balance.

Post a Record

In the study area, post the following four things.

1. The Study Guide.
2. The graph showing the homework period required and the actual study time for each day.
3. The Reward Table listing the rewards which can be earned for each success, and the amount of reward a success is worth, or the number of successes required for a reward.
4. The Success Sheet showing how many successes have been earned and not spent for a reward.

Final Comments

Whether or not the child does his or her homework is "optional." The parents should never instruct the child to do the homework, or reprimand, cajole, urge, threaten, or do anything else of this nature to get the student to work.

You should be very matter-of-fact or businesslike about homework. It may take a while before you note any effects. The attitude must be "Here are the consequences—take it or leave it." That is, other than setting up the program, you leave all responsibility to the child.

Avoid any argument over the program with the child. If he or she does not like the rules or regulations set up, just say that this is the way it is, take it or leave it. If the child continues to argue, tell him or her you have things to do and *leave*. Do this consistently.

Successes should be praised and long-term improvement appreciated. However, ignore failures or "no games."

Good luck! With patience and precision, you will soon solve the homework problem.

STUDY GUIDE

Study location:＿＿＿＿＿＿＿＿＿＿＿＿＿＿＿＿＿＿＿＿＿＿＿

How long to study:＿＿＿＿＿＿＿＿＿＿＿＿＿＿＿＿＿＿＿＿＿

Time to start homework:＿＿＿＿＿＿＿＿＿＿＿＿＿＿＿＿＿＿

Days to do homework:＿＿＿＿＿＿＿＿＿＿＿＿＿＿＿＿＿＿＿

INSTRUCTIONS: Fill out this form when you start the homework program. As you go along, make changes required in the extra space provided.

REWARD TABLE

Reward & How Much	Number of Successes to Get It

THE GOOD KID BOOK

SUCCESS SHEET

Prior Balance	New	Spent	For	New Balance

7.
Dealing with Dawdling

"DAWDLING" is a rather vague term which refers to a great many things children do. Undoubtedly, twenty parents would have twenty different definitions, and ten times this number of illustrations. In this chapter we are not discussing refusals to do a specific task assigned or some task which the child is supposed to do regularly. If your child actually does not fulfill requests, you should use the program in Chapter 1. This chapter deals with a child who does what is expected, but slowly, late, or casually.

Have you ever wondered how anybody could take so long to get ready for bed? Suddenly, a thousand small tasks arise, as if by magic. Homework which has been forgotten for days suddenly needs to be looked at, or books and papers need to be collected. Cleaning the room, usually ignored, becomes a high-priority activity; toys need to be put away, favorite objects need to be found, and those long-lost slippers need to be searched for. And how about those last-minute phone calls before getting ready? Shoes come off as if in slow motion, and ten minutes of other activity intervene between the left one and the right one. Another frequent symptom is a dreaming, trancelike attitude. If it isn't getting ready for bed it may be dressing or undressing, setting the table, taking out the garbage, cleaning up, or coming when called. Typically, either the child does not do the task in a reasonable length of time, or the child engages in various other minor activities, such as playing with something, looking at a book or magazine, talking, mild complaining, restlessness, and so forth, instead of doing the assigned task.

This chapter does *not* cover situations in which there is any question of the child's ability to perform the task. It is assumed that sometimes the child does the required job in a reasonable amount of time, so it is known that he or she can do what is required. The program also does not cover situations in which the child is slow only occasionally for some specific reason.

Dawdling is another problem which deserves attention more because of the way it affects the family than because it is itself serious or dangerous. Constant arguing and bickering are not fruitful. Solving the dawdling problem can reduce this bickering and may be one step toward a more positive relationship.

How to Begin

Read the entire program yourself. If other adults in your household will help in carrying out the program, have them read it also. Make sure you all agree on and understand the program before going further.

The first step is to make sure that the problem is really with your child. It is very easy for an adult to become impatient and to want things done at once when in fact there is no necessity for speed, and possibly not enough time to get things done. There are two guidelines you can use.

Necessity. At times you feel your child dawdles. Is there any actual reason for getting things done quickly? If dawdling when getting ready for school causes lateness, more speed is necessary. However, if the child would get ready on time even at his or her own slow pace there is no necessity. Perhaps by recognizing the lack of necessity you will be able to tolerate the slowness better, and let your child choose the pace. Similarly, if your child's slowness in setting the table or some other task makes other people late or inconveniences others, there is some necessity for speeding things up. If not, perhaps the problem is yours, not the child's.

Possibility. Occasionally, we may not realize how much time certain things actually take. If your child works steadily but still does not get through when you feel he or she should, it may be that your estimates of how fast the child can go need revising.

Discuss the family problems you have with dawdling with your child, with other adults in the household (if any), and with other parents you know. With each, decide on the necessity for and possibility of your child doing things faster. In each discussion, check the boxes below which seem appropriate. Check the box under "Necessity" if as a result of that discussion you feel that more speed is

necessary. Check the box under "Possibility" if as a result of that discussion you feel that there is enough time available to make faster results possible. Do this for each discussion.

	Necessity	Possibility
Discussion with my child	_____	_____
Discussion with another parent	_____	_____
Discussion with other adults at home (cross out boxes if there are no other adults)	_____	_____

If you could not check all or most of the applicable boxes, perhaps you should not carry out this program. This is for you to decide. If you did, here is the program.

Basic Idea

The procedure is based upon the assumption that children dawdle for one or more of the following reasons:

1. Dawdling gets attention from adults.
2. Children avoid having to do something unpleasant by dawdling.
3. The consequences of doing the job promptly or slowly are identical.

Attention. There are a lot of ways we give children attention when they dawdle. Do you "bug" your child when dawdling occurs? Do you constantly remind the child of the task? Do you come over to try and be helpful with suggestions? All this is attention.

Avoidance. Children often are quite clever at using dawdling to avoid things. Do you ever tell your child to "forget it" when the child dawdles over something you know he or she can do quite well? Or perhaps you do a part of the task for your child. Have you ever told a child to forget some other chore because a first one took such a long time? Have you done this even when the slowness was due to dawdling, not because the task was a long or hard one? If so, you understand that dawdling works.

Consequences. Do you take it for granted when your child does a task promptly—that is, not thank him or show your appreciation? Regardless of whether the task is done reasonably fast or dragged out forever? If so, the result of doing things promptly is the same as doing them slowly. Promptness and dawdling have the same consequence.

For each of three sections above, circle the heading if you feel it applies to your situation. The program attempts to do the following:

1. Remove the attention-getting value of dawdling.
2. Remove the rewards for dawdling by not letting children avoid chores by dawdling.
3. Provide naturally occurring pleasant consequences for getting done compared with less pleasant consequences for dawdling.

Choose Your Target Behavior

In this program you will work on only one type of dawdling behavior at a time. As the child improves in one area, you can deal with a second problem. You will teach your child to be more prompt with all tasks, until you no longer feel that dawdling is a problem worth worrying about.

1. *Make a list.* Write down problem areas which concern you. Is getting up in the morning one? Is eating at meals one? Perhaps cleaning the room or doing some other chore is a problem. Whatever they are, jot them down. Then discuss them with the child.
2. *Can the child do it?* Now look your list over, and ask yourself the following question about each item: "Am I absolutely sure that the child can do this task?" There is only one way you can be sure, and that is if the child does do the task sometimes, even if rarely. Cross out those tasks for which there really is a question as to whether or not the child has actually learned to do what is required.
3. *Proper wording.* Now look at how you have worded the remaining items in the list. They should be worded so they physically describe what the child is to do without value judgments or opinions. For instance, do not write ". . . a good job cleaning up his room," because what two people call a good job might not be the same. Instead, describe exactly what you want by its physical description. For instance, change a "good job" to "all clothes and toys are in either closet, dresser, or bookshelf." This is what you mean by a good job. Reward all things that might require a judgment.
4. *Ranking your problems.* Now decide which of these types of dawdling behavior bothers you the most. Write the number 1 before it, and write 2 and 3 before the next two worst, and so forth.
5. *How slow is dawdling?* Your next task is to decide on a reason-

able amount of time for accomplishing each chore. Be generous, and write the amount of time you think the child should take for each of the three biggest problems you listed.

6. *Rewrite your list.* At the end of this chapter there is a Dawdling List. Rewrite your list on this form. Write the first ranked, or most important, problem first, then the next, and so on. For the first three, fill in the time limits you decided upon.

Talking to the Child

We are all affected by how we are spoken to, as well as by what is said. This is as true of a child as of an adult. In this program, there are five guides for talking to the child. If you can remember the name OSCAR you can remember the rules.

O—*Once or twice.* When you ask the child to do one of the tasks on which he or she usually dawdles, ask only once or twice.

S—*Specify.* When you give the child an instruction, specify exactly what you want the child to do. Say "Please take out the garbage" rather than "Please do your job." Always make your instruction factual, and have it describe what you want done.

C—*Casual.* Speak in a casual and matter-of-fact way. Sound as if you assume that the child will do as you ask, not as if you expect resistance and are already preparing for a fight. Don't make any threats or promises. "Please take out the garbage" is therefore preferred to "Won't you ever take out the garbage?"

A—*Annoy.* If the child does not do the job, do not annoy, nag, or "bug" him or her about it. Instead, ignore the child.

R—*Reward.* If the child does as you have asked, reward him or her with some praise or word of appreciation. We all can use a bit of encouragement or recognition.

Memorize the rules so that you can use them in practice.

Remove Attention

This is mainly a list of "don'ts." Because you don't want to give your child attention when he dawdles,

• Don't remind, nag, bug, prompt, or suggest more than once or twice.
• Don't scold, threaten, or punish.

- Don't ask what is wrong, if help is needed, or make sarcastic comments.
- Don't provide help unless you are sure your child cannot do the task himself.
- Don't stand and watch!

Natural Consequences

Try to arrange "natural" unpleasant consequences for not performing on time. For example, if a child does not dress or undress, and this means the child is late for school, misses some activity, or cannot go someplace, fine. A child who does not do mealtime chores (e.g., setting the table) might not share in the meal—he or she could eat alone or not at all. If a child does not come when called, especially for something such as meals or activities the child enjoys, start without the child or let him or her miss it.

As indicated above, try to arrange it so "good" things follow doing the task at which the child dawdles. Dinner can be arranged to follow garbage emptying. You can always thank, praise, or compliment.

Even though you are starting with only the first type of behavior, list below natural consequences for dawdling for the first three tasks you selected. In your program, arrange things so these consequences will follow dawdling in a matter-of-fact way.

1. _____

_____

2. _____

_____

3. _____

_____

Don't Let Dawdling Be a Way to Avoid Unpleasant Tasks

Where it is possible, do not let the child avoid the task by dawdling. Do not do the job for the child unless it is absolutely necessary. In most cases, this rule will be easy to follow.

Wait

A major reason many children dawdle is that adults are so impatient. Finally, adults do the job for the dawdler. It is easier to do the job yourself than to wait for the child. Both of you suffer from this.

Wait for the child. When the child is slow do not become impatient and do the job yourself. If possible do not let the child go on to another activity without completing the task. Often you can arrange things to make this easier. One way was mentioned—using natural consequences. For instance, if your son is to take out the garbage, ask him to do it five minutes before dinner. If he has not done it by dinner, matter-of-factly tell him that when the garbage is emptied he can eat. Don't hold up the meal for him; if he misses the first course, he misses it.

Moving On

Work on the first dawdling behavior alone until you feel it is no longer a problem. Then continue the program for this type of behavior, but start it for the second also. When this is no longer a problem, start the program for the third, keeping the program going for all three. After you have solved three, you will be expert enough to decide if you want to do more. Keep an informal record of progress on the form which follows.

	Program Started (Date)	*Program Successful* (Date)
Behavior 1		
Behavior 2		
Behavior 3		

In addition, each day score yourself a plus or a minus to see if you have followed all the program suggestions. If your program is working, you will probably have plus signs in most of the boxes. If you do not, your program probably is not working.

Once or twice																			
Specify																			
Casual																			
Annoy																			
Reward																			
Natural consequences																			
Remove attention																			
No avoidance																			
Waiting																			

Final Comments

You may have noticed that the suggestions in the chapter are based on many of the same principles as those for other problems. Being reasonable is always important. Being reasonable usually is very close to being realistic. Another principle is that of providing appropriate consequences. This program uses mainly natural consequences, plus praise and approval. It also tries to avoid having rewards occur after undesirable behavior—that is, you try to prevent your child from getting attention or avoiding tasks by dawdling. You also attempt to give your child a chance to perform properly, by waiting, not repeating instructions, and so on. These techniques are good for many problems. They will help your child to develop skills and a positive, pleasant manner.

DAWDLING LIST

Write dawdling problems on this list in order of importance. For the first three also list reasonable time limits. As you work on new problems, write in time limits for them.

Number	Problem	Time Limit
1		
2		
3		
4		
5		
6		
7		
8		
9		
10		

8.
A Bedtime Story

"**W**E can never get Sam to go to bed on time." "Mary gets out of bed at least six times within thirty minutes of having her light turned out." "When we tell Carlos to get ready for bed he argues and argues." "She just won't go to sleep unless one of us sits in her room for hours." "We have to remind him to get ready for bed a hundred times a night." "Angela won't go to sleep without that light on."

If these statements sound familiar to you, remember that most parents have occasional bedtime problems with their children. Frequent problems are not at all unusual. Bedtime should be a pleasant relaxing time which prepares children for a good sleep and for the next day, and at which parents and children have a short time to talk and be together. Why is bedtime frequently a problem, and what can be done about it?

Causes of Bedtime Problems

Many people feel that children have bedtime problems because of various fears, emotional problems, or psychological or family disturbances. I have found that the majority of bedtime problems are not directly related to difficulties of this sort. However, it is not difficult to see how emotional explanations for bedtime problems develop. One frequent situation is when in the past a child has had some actual problem, whether it was an unpleasant experience one evening or a school or home problem. Because the child really was upset at this time and therefore had a temporary problem with bedtime, parents were very lenient about making the child go to bed or gave the child special attention. However, when bedtime problems continue after the temporary upset no longer exists, it is usually due to the special attention the parents had provided at bedtime; as a result of this attention the child learns to have continuing bedtime difficulties. When the child now has prolonged bedtime problems the parents attribute the difficulties to the original upsetting situation (e.g., they think the child has developed a fear of the dark), when in fact the parents' reactions to this situation are the problems.

The second situation arises when merely as a result of parental attention a child learns to procrastinate, resist going to bed, demand his parents' presence after lights out, and the like. Eventually, this leads to a hassle over bedtime. As a result of the frequent hassle the child becomes upset over going to bed. The parents then believe that the child has bedtime problems because he is upset, when actually he is upset because of the bedtime problems.

The basic reason for continued or prolonged bedtime problems in most cases is usually one of the items on the following list. If you feel that any of these factors fit your situation you might circle the appropriate number.

1. *Having problems lets the child stay up later.* Many children enjoy the thing they can do in the evening, such as being with other family members, playing, reading, or watching TV. By arguing, prolonging getting ready for bed, and dawdling over bedtime the children stay up later and enjoy more of these things.

1. *Arguing and procrastinating get parent attention.* This takes many forms. Parents may keep reminding children to go to bed, cajole them, bribe them, or just spend a lot of time trying to get them into bed. This attention seems to reward a child for bedtime problem behavior, and the behavior persists.

3. *Children get attention by getting out of bed often.* This is nearly the same as reason 2. By popping in and out of bed a number of times children get to see family members, see what is going on, and often to take part or interact in some way. This rewards getting up.

4. *Children are rewarded for crying or "fearful" behavior by having a parent stay with them.* Many parents inadvertently teach their children to have fears or to cry at bedtime by staying in the room for a long time with a child who is already in bed. Each time the child cries or complains, the parents come in again. This attention is usually the reason the child continues to cry or to act afraid.

Usually, children do not plan the above things to get parental

attention or to prolong enjoyable activities. Just as parents may not realize they are teaching their children to have bedtime problems, children do not realize they are learning this behavior. Regardless of intent, though, these consequences teach children bad habits.

These bedtime problems can usually be solved with patience and consistency. To do so requires correctly preparing the child to go to bed, and making good bedtime behavior more rewarding than problem bedtime behavior. This program will teach you one way to do this.

Whom Is This Program For?

If you have a child who has any of the bedtime problems described at the beginning of this chapter, and is a toddler or in elementary school, this program may help you. Parts of the program will also work with infants who have learned to cry and to resist sleep unless parents stay in the room.

The procedures are not designed for the child who has never had bedtime problems and who suddenly develops them. Abrupt development of bedtime problems suggests that something has changed in the child's life, and the first step should be to try to find out what this is and correct it. Of course, in addition you should try to avoid doing any of the things which will cause difficulties to persist.

How to Start

Before starting, read the entire chapter. Make sure any other family members who have anything to do with the child's going to bed also read the chapter. Then go back over the chapter, starting with the next section, and put it into action one step at a time.

Preparing for Bedtime

Everyone has an easier time going to sleep after a relaxed and pleasant evening. Tension, problems, or a lot of work just before going to bed do not promote a good sleep, and in children may lead to avoidance or fear of bedtime. Here are some suggestions to promote a better atmosphere for bedtime.

1. *Chores.* Rearrange children's chores or tasks so they do not have to do them within an hour before going to bed. If there are tasks which a child with bedtime problems usually does just before bedtime, change the schedule so the work is done at some earlier time.

2. *Homework.* Homework should be treated like other chores. Rearrange the child's schedule so that homework is completed at least an hour before bedtime. A child who has regular trouble doing his homework may worry about school after getting into bed. If your child has homework difficulties which may be contributing to bedtime problems, read Chapter 6 on homework problems and try to solve this problem as well.

3. *Critical discussions or punishments.* If you feel that your child's behavior needs correction or punishment, do not discuss this problem or punish the child within two hours of bedtime. Try to arrange such discussion for an earlier time during the day, perhaps immediately after dinner. Obviously, being upset at bedtime will not help.

4. *Fights.* If your child frequently gets into fights or arguments with other family members, try to prevent these from occurring within two hours of bedtime. If need be, you can separate the individuals involved, provide other activities which will take up this time, or interrupt such behavior and suggest that the issue be resolved some other time. If fighting is a major problem with your children you might consult Chapter 5 on resolving fighting, arguing, and teasing.

5. *Other exciting activities.* Some children, particularly young children, may get quite keyed up from exciting TV shows or movies. Other children do not seem bothered by these things and calm down easily. If you feel that such events just before bedtime may be contributing to bedtime problems, try to rearrange the schedule so that calmer activities occur in the thirty minutes before bedtime.

6. *Pleasant relaxation.* All of the above problems can be avoided or minimized by a planned period of pleasant relaxation called "Relax Time" for a child just before bedtime. This is especially true for younger children. Such a period need only last fifteen to thirty minutes. This time can be taken up with a warm bath, a bedtime story, quiet games in bed (such as board games), reading in bed, or other calming activities.

Later in this chapter I will describe the way in which you will use the Relax Time.

The Bedtime Game

The Bedtime Game is a method of making going to bed properly more fun than procrastinating, arguing, or listening to reminders. The game consists of three parts.

Bedtime Game Board. At the end of this chapter is the Bedtime

Game Board. This is like most board games; if the child does certain things he is allowed to make moves on the board. The child can make three moves per night. One move is allowed for each of the following:

- Getting read for bed with only one reminder and no arguments.
- Using the Relax Time.
- Being in bed with lights out on time (unless there is a special "lights out" program as described later).

At night, just before turning off the lights and leaving the child, the parent tells the child how many moves he or she has earned. You can use a thumbtack or a pin as a marker to make the moves on the board. On the first day the marker is placed in the "Start" box. That night, any moves earned are made. Each night, additional earned moves are made and the child slowly progresses around the board from the start box to the finish box. Whenever the child's marker passes or lands on a prize spot, one surprise can be drawn from the Surprise Pack, which will be described. As you will see, it is possible to earn more than one surprise on certain nights, and to not earn any surprise on other nights, even though the child performed well.

The Game Card. At the end of this chapter is the Game Card. This is a card you post on your child's bedroom door to remind the child of how moves may be made and surprises earned. In the blank following "Being in bed with lights out by . . ." write in your child's bedtime. In the blank before this for the relax time write in a time fifteen to thirty minutes earlier than the bedtime hour.

The Surprise Pack. The Surprise Pack is a paper bag, box, cloth bag, or other container in which you will put slips of paper listing the surprises that your child may earn. It should be large enough so that your child can reach into it and draw out a slip of paper without seeing what is on the paper until it is out. You may decorate the Surprise Pack to appeal to your child. Put the Surprise Pack Card (at the end of the chapter) on the "Surprise Pack" with glue, staples, or tape. The Surprise Pack should be kept next to your child's bed.

In the Surprise Pack you will put fifty 2x2-inch pieces of paper folded in quarters. Each will have a surprise written on it, and you should fold the papers so the writing cannot be seen. Exact instructions are given later.

Some of the surprises you will decide upon with your child. Some you will make up without your child's knowledge.

Before you start the program with your child you will need to do the following.

1. Make and decorate a Surprise Pack.
2. Put the Surprise Pack Card on the Surprise Pack.
3. Look at the Surprise List at the end of the chapter. It is the worksheet you use before making final decisions on what surprises will be in the Surprise Pack. It is for suggestions, not final ideas which will be in the pack. You will note that it has spaces for daily surprises, weekly surprises, and twice-a-month surprises. Now, before talking with your child, write on this list your ideas.

   Daily surprises are things our child can earn every day. Here are some suggestions for daily surprises; write on the list under "Daily Surprises" any that seem appropriate for your child, plus any ideas you have.

- Ten minutes extra bedtime.
- Mom or Dad will read me a story for ten minutes.
- Mom or Dad will play a game with me for ten minutes.
- Bubble bath.

Weekly surprises are things your child can earn about once a week. Make up your own suggestions and use the list below for ideas. Make sure you write these ideas under "Weekly Surprises."

- Stay up and watch an extra TV program.
- Mom or Dad will take out the garbage for me (or some other chore).
- Mom or Dad will serve me breakfast in bed.
- At dinner, Mom or Dad will wear a funny costume I make up.
- Bonus on allowance of____(you write in amount).

Here are some suggestions for the "Twice-a-Month" section.

- Special trip (write what it is).
- Go to a movie within a week.
- Day off from all chores.

You will note that there are spaces for many suggestions. Later on in this program you will also get suggestions from your child. From the complete Surprise List which will include your suggestions and your child's you will select some to write on papers and put in the Surprise Pack. When you have written your suggestions on the Surprise List, go on to the next section.

Starting the Bedtime Game

Here are the few simple steps required to start the Bedtime Game. Just follow them in order, and check each as you complete it. However, first follow the directions given earlier for preparing for bedtime.

1. Meet with your child. Explain that you have decided to help your child go to bed on time with fewer problems by making bedtime more fun.

2. Show your child the Game Card. Explain that your child will be able to make moves on the Game Board by doing the things on the card. Tell your child that you will give only one reminder a night that bedtime is coming. Explain that your child will be able to make a move and perhaps earn one or two surprises by getting ready for bed with only one reminder and with no arguments. Explain about Relax Time. Tell your child that getting into bed and doing one of the Relax Time activities by the time indicated will earn a bonus move. Tell your child that still another move on the Game Board can be earned by having lights out by the time listed on the Game Card. Say that each move might win a surprise. Tape or thumbtack the Game Card to your child's bedroom door.

3. Now show your child the Game Board. Tell the child that each move earned for the things on the Game Card will mean that the marker can move one space. Explain that the child will be able to take one surprise out of the Surprise Pack whenever the marker passes or lands on the proper space. Explain that on some nights your child may earn no surprises, and on some perhaps one or more. Tell your child that although most of the surprises are little, some are bigger. Post the Game Board near your child's bed.

4. Show your child the decorated Surprise Pack with its card on it. Tell him or her that the surprises will be written on pieces of paper in the pack, and that when the marker moves onto or past a surprise space the child will be able to draw one surprise out of the pack. Tell the child that you have some ideas for surprises, and describe one or two surprises you have thought up that may be put into the pack. Tell your child that you have other ideas which you are keeping secret so they will be real surprises. Then ask your child for ideas for surprises. Encourage the child to think up ideas, giving more illustrations if neces-

sary. As your child gives you appropriate ideas, write them on the Surprise List. Make a judgment about whether these surprises should be daily, weekly, or twice a month, and write them under the correct heading. Then tell your child that you are going to put the surprises on pieces of paper and put them into the pack. Tell your child that some of the surprises will be things he or she suggested, that some may be the ones you mentioned, and that some will be complete surprises that you are not going to describe until they are earned.

5. *Without* your child, look over the complete Surprise List. Mark what you judge to be the eight best daily surprises. Write each of these eight on five pieces of paper, fold them, and put them in the pack. This gives forty surprises in the pack.

Then look over the weekly surprises. Mark what you feel are the four best. Write each of them on two pieces of paper, and fold these eight papers and put them in the pack. With these eight there are now forty-eight surprises in the pack.

Now look over the twice-a-month suggestions. Pick the two best of these, write them each on one piece of paper, and place them in the pack. You now have fifty surprises in the pack, although some of them are repeats. There are a lot more daily surprises than weekly or twice-a-month surprises. Keep your Surprise List in case you want to add new things to the pack or take out old ones.

6. Bring the Surprise Pack back to your child's room. Shake it up. Let your child reach in and feel the papers. Have the child draw one out and read it (or read it to the child). If it is one your child does not seem to like, let the child draw out and look at another. As soon as the child gets one he or she seems to like, put all the papers back in the pack. Shake it up again, and put it by the child's bed. Tell your child that each time a surprise is earned on the game board by good bedtime behavior he or she will be able to reach in the pack and get a surprise. Tell the child that you will try to provide the surprise as soon as possible. Explain that some surprises are bigger than others.

Carrying Out the Bedtime Game

1. Each night, about fifteen to thirty minutes before the Relax Time, tell your child it is so many minutes to Relax Time, and so many minutes to bedtime.

2. Do not argue or remind the child again, until bedtime has passed. Ignore any arguments.
3. If the child is in bed by bedtime, come in, tell the child what things the child has earned moves for, and make the moves for the child or let the child make them on the Game Board. If the child earns any surprises let the child pick them right away. Shake the pack and let the child reach in. Have the child read the surprise, or read it yourself.
4. Tell the child when you will be able to deliver the surprises. For something like later bedtime or a story, it should be the next night, if possible. For other things, give the child some estimate of when the reward will be delivered. The child should keep the slip until the surprise is delivered. Then fold the slip, put it back in the pack, and shake the pack up.
5. If your child is in bed on time, praise and compliment him or her whether or not a surprise was earned. If the child is not in bed on time you may give extra reminders after bedtime. When the child gets in bed, just say good night warmly. Do not comment on the Bedtime Game.

Changing and Ending the Game

- If you have new ideas for surprises, or some do not seem to work, feel free to add or delete things in the pack. Keep the same number of daily, weekly, and bimonthly surprises.
- Feel free to change Bedtimes or Relax Times if experience suggests they are not reasonable. Make sure you change the Game Card.
- If after two weeks your child does well, but still argues, change the Game Card so your child earns two moves if he is in bed on time with only one reminder and no arguments. Give *no* moves for getting in bed on time with arguments or extra reminders.
- If your child finishes the board, you may start over or just stop the game. Make a judgment by seeing how well things are going.

The Child Who Gets Out of Bed Too Often

There are some bedtime problems not covered by the game. One of these is the child who gets out of bed an inordinate number of times after lights out. If your child does this, and you want to change it, use this part of the program. If getting into bed on time is also a problem you may follow the procedures in this section and use the Bedtime Game at the same time. In either case, follow the instructions for preparing for bed.

Most children who get into and out of bed a lot of times do so because of the attention they receive. If you are correctly preparing the child for bedtime (as described earlier) it is very unlikely that your child gets in and out of bed because of some "need for reassurance." The best reassurance and security you can give your child is to provide a generally relaxed atmosphere, and within that framework make clear that you care about his welfare. Providing firm, reasonable guidelines concerning sleep helps do this.

Since getting in and out of bed is a device for attracting attention, it is important to avoid giving that attention.

Step 1. If you are not using the Bedtime Game, follow the directions under "Preparing for Bedtime" until all has gone well for at least a week. Just provide the relaxation period for the child in an informal manner, and suggest that the child use it. If the child does, fine; if not, just ignore it.

If you are using the Bedtime Game, start the entire game procedure, including "Preparing for Bed," for at least a week before starting Step 2 of this procedure. If the Bedtime Game is not going well, continue for a longer period before starting Step 2. In other words, keep up with the Bedtime Game until it is going fairly routinely for at least a week.

Whether or not you are using the Bedtime Game you should shut the child's door after the child is in bed with the lights out.

Step 2. The goal of this step is to make sure that when your child does get out of bed after bedtime, he or she does not talk to anyone or see anything interesting happening. How easy this is to do will depend upon the physical arrangement of your home. If the child's bedroom door opens into a living room or family room it will be more difficult than if the child's bedroom is on another floor or down a hall from where the action is.

Try to arrange it so that no one is near the bedroom area for about an hour after the child goes to bed. This may require some rearrangement of your usual evening activities. Do the best you can. In any case, this change will be only temporary. Remember, the bedroom door should be shut.

When you have made these arrangements and put them into action for a night, you are ready to start Step 3.

Step 3. Step 3 is very difficult for many people. It involves ignoring the child when the child gets out of bed after bedtime. If you are in another room and the child says something or yells or asks a question, just ignore it. If the child comes into the room you are in, everyone there should do the same thing. However, to make this more natural and reasonable, you may go through the following steps:

1. *First night of the program.* The first two times the child comes out and talks to you and yells a question or whatever, you may say, "We are not going to talk to you after you are in bed. You need your sleep. Ask me in the morning, and now go back to bed." Ignore any further comments the child makes, or anything the child does, including crying.

2. *Second night of the program.* Respond the first time the child asks for attention with a comment, as on the first night. After this first time, do not respond at all.

3. *Third and later nights of the program.* Ignore the child from the first time. If the child gets up or talks or makes noise, do not respond in any way.

If the child does not shut the bedroom door after returning, shut it yourself with no comment.

Ignoring the child is very difficult for some people. However, the success of the program depends heavily upon how well you can do this. If you respond to the child you are helping to teach the child even stronger bad sleep habits. By ignoring the child you are helping the child learn to go quickly to sleep and have a healthy night's sleep. Obviously, if the child presents you with a new and real emergency, do not follow the program, but take care of the trouble.

For most parents, Step 3 of this program will solve the problem wthin two weeks. However, if you have carried out the program exactly and still have problems you may go to Step 4.

Step 4. By this point, you have tried reasonable procedures for several weeks. If these do not work it may be necessary to resort to a carefully controlled version of that old parental favorite, spanking.

As a general rule it is wise to use as little punishment of any sort as possible. However, properly used punishment sometimes seems to be the best option available. First, if used properly it usually works quickly, and prevents exposing the child to long-drawn-out arguments and parental disfavor. Second, if the problem is one which is not good for the child the punishment may be better for the child than the problem. Read the section below on how to use spanking and decide if you wish to try Step 4. If you do not, continue Step 3 even more rigorously for a longer period of time.

When to spank. As noted, you only go to Step 4 if you have given Step 3 a long and consistent try. Step 4 should not be used unless this is the case.

After the child has been put into bed and the door has been closed, allow the child to come out of the room once. Ignore this the first time, as you did in Step 3.

The second time the child comes out of the room, you spank the child. However, it is important to follow the guidelines for spanking given in the next section.

How to spank. There are several rules you should follow in administering the spanking. These are designed to avoid any bad effects of spanking and to ensure that the spanking procedure will work.

1. Spank the child the moment the child comes out of the bedroom. Combined with the procedures you have carried out so far, this will make sure that the child understands the spanking. The sooner you can spank the child after the child comes out of the room, the better.

2. The first two times you spank the child, make a brief statement such as "You know you are supposed to stay in your room and go to sleep." Do not have any other conversation with the child. After the second time, whether both times occur in the same or on different nights, spank the child without comment. This is to reduce any effects of attention.

3. After you spank the child, gently but firmly and without comment put the child in the bedroom and shut the door.

4. The spanking should not be so soft that it amounts to a social event. Nor should it be so hard or long that it is a beating or damages the child in any way. We have found that a good rule is four smacks with an open hand on the bottom. If the smacks are so soft that your hand does not sting at all immediately after the spanking (unless your hand is callused) the spanking was too soft. If your hand still stings about a minute after the spanking, it was too hard. The spanking should be just hard enough to hurt, *and no harder.*

5. While you are doing this procedure you should not use spankings for any other behavior of the child.

It is very important to continue having a pleasant preparation for bed period during Step 4. In the morning, you must make a point of interacting pleasantly with the child. If the child went to bed the night before without getting up more than once you should praise the child lavishly.

After five nights in a row in which the child does not get up more than once, and thus does not receive a spanking, praise the child for improvement and go back to Step 3. However, if things get worse again use the same guidelines to start Step 4 once more. In the spaces provided on the chart which follows, record how many times the child gets up each night.

NIGHT

1	2	3	4	5	6	7	8	9	10	11	12	13	14

Each night, make a mark in the box each time the child gets up.

If the number of times your child gets up after being put into bed is not half the number by Day 10 that it was on Day 1, discontinue Step 4. Follow the rule for going back to Step 3, which was described earlier. Check each item below until you check one of the final two items.

_____ I am using Step 4.

_____ I am doing the preparation for bedtime.

_____ I am spanking the child immediately after the child gets up.

_____ Other than the first two times in Step 4, I am not conversing with the child.

_____ After the spanking I am putting the child in the bedroom and shutting the door.

_____ I am spanking with an open hand four times.

_____ I am spanking just hard enough to hurt and not harder or softer.

_____ I am not spanking the child for other behavior.

_____ I am finishing Step 4 because my child has not gotten up more than once for five days in a row.

_____ I am finishing Step 4 because after ten days the child is still getting up more than half as much as on Day 1.

If you have not had success with Step 3 and/or Step 4, it is probable that you will not solve this problem without outside help or additional time. Most parents who carry this program out consist-ently are successful. However, sometimes parents find it difficult to be sufficiently patient and consistent. If you are one of the few parents for whom this has been a problem there are several options available. See if any of the following suggestions seem useful.

1. Seek professional help from a psychologist, psychiatrist, or social worker. Tell the professional you are trying to solve this problem but are having difficulties carrying out the program con-sistently. Some professionals will provide consultation in your home on such problems. Your local child guidance clinic, mental health clinic, or university may be able to provide such a person.

2. If you are sure your problem has been your inability to be con-sistent, you may have a relative or friend who you feel is a calm, kind, and consistent person, and who would be willing to spend a few evenings helping you get this problem under control. If so, go over the program with this person and see if you both feel this would be a reasonable thing to do.

3. Sometimes one parent is more sensitive to children's crying or asking questions than the other. Often, having one person start the program while the other stays out of the house for several evenings solves what seems like an otherwise difficult problem.

We Have to Stay in the Child's Room Until the Child Is Asleep

This program is very simple, and related to the program for the child who comes out of the bedroom often. Some children, especially some young toddlers or infants, cry the minute an adult leaves the room at bedtime. Many parents keep coming back in the room, leav-ing, and returning again when the baby or child cries. Some hold and coddle the child. If this persists the explanation is the same as that given in the last section: Attention teaches the child to cry.

To solve this problem, put the child in bed, going through the bed-preparation procedure as was described in the last section, shut the door, and leave. *Do not come back.* That is the hard part. Some chil-dren, for the first three to five nights, will sound pitiful, and some parents fear that neighbors will think they are beating their child. But this is the best cure, and the best way to end the long-drawn-out epi-sodes that leave both child and parents absolutely exhausted.

It is very important not to start this program unless you will stick with it. Why is this? Imagine the following typical situation. Mr. and Mrs. Carpenter decide that they will follow this program and end the hours of sitting in the baby's room, holding the baby, and going in and out as the baby cries. So for two nights they stick to the program. On the third the baby cries louder, harder, and longer than usual, and they relent. What has the baby learned? The original loudness and length of crying was not rewarded with the parents' presence, but on the third night louder and longer crying was. So all they have done is teach the baby to cry louder and longer. By starting and then stopping when things got rough, they have made the situation worse than ever. And, unfortunately, with this problem things usually get worse before they get better. So before starting, be warned—and make a careful decision.

If you are very determined to end this problem but feel that you will not be successful in sticking with it through the first five days, there is an option. If you have a relative or close friend whom you trust completely, and who you are sure is less likely to get upset than you, perhaps the friend can start things for you for the first five days. If you wish to do this, talk with the friend and have the friend read this entire section. Then you and the friend can come to a mutual decision.

To help you tell how things are going, a graph is provided at the end of this chapter. On the graph, record the length of time between putting the child to bed and hearing the last cry or yell. A whimper or a groan from the sleeping child does not count. A worksheet is provided to help you figure things out. On the worksheet, write in the first column after the date the exact time that you put the child in bed. Then each time the child cries, write down the time the crying stops. When twenty minutes go by without any cries or yells, stop recording. Then subtract the bedtime from the time the crying or yelling stopped. This is the length of time the child cried or yelled that night. Put this on the graph.

A sample is filled out on the worksheet and the graph. You will note that the date on the sample was 11/23. The child was put to bed at 8:15. The child started crying and yelling a short time after being put in bed and ended at 8:50. Soon, the child started again, and ended at 9.03. The child started again and ended at 9:12. The child started again and ended at 9:25. As the child did not cry again before twenty minutes were up no further record was kept. As the child was put into bed at 8:15 and ended at 9:25, seventy minutes went by

before the child stopped crying for twenty minutes. This seventy minutes was recorded on the graph. The rest of the worksheet and the
graph are for you to use. Remember, for the first two to five days
things may get worse. Within ten days you should see a definite improvement with hardly any crying or yelling. In the rare event this is
not the case, and you are sure that nobody has been going into the
child's room when the child cries or yells, you are one of the very few
parents for whom this program will not work, and you should discontinue it.

If you have trouble getting your child to go to bed, and the child
is old enough, you can use this program along with the bedtime game.

My Child Will Not Go to Sleep Without a Light On

Many children will not go to sleep at night without a light on. One
major question that needs to be answered is why this is a problem.
Obviously, if it appears to keep the child awake for a long time after
bedtime it is a problem. If it uses more electricity than seems warranted it may be a problem. If the light bothers other people it is also
a problem. There may be individual reasons in some families besides
these that make it a problem. But sleeping with a light is not in itself
a problem; it has no known bad effects even if it is not "outgrown,"
although it usually is eventually.

If you are sure the light is a problem, here is a simple way to take
care of it. Check each step as it is completed.

_____ 1. If there are other sleep problems, consult the appropriate
sections of this chapter and take care of them first.

_____ 2. Use the procedures under "Preparing for Bedtime" for a
week without doing anything about the light.

_____ 3. If the light which remains on contains more than one bulb,
remove all but one bulb. Put plug taps or burned-out bulbs
in the socket so the child cannot get a shock.

_____ 4. Reduce the size of the light bulb, depending upon what is
used, every other night according to the schedule below
until a 25-watt light bulb is used. Leave the 25-watt bulb
in for three nights.

      a. Over 100 watts—reduce to 100

      b. 75 watts

      c. 60 watts

   d. 40 watts
   e. 25 watts

_____ 5. If the bulb which is left on is in a ceiling or wall fixture, put the 25-watt bulb in a small lamp instead and leave this on for three nights. Put a bulb in the fixture but leave it off at night. The lamp should be located so it lights up the room about as much as the ceiling or wall light did. (If you started with a lamp, skip this step.)

_____ 6. Move the lamp so that it cannot be seen directly from the bed. Leave this for three nights. (If the lamp started in this location skip this step.)

_____ 7. Get a night light that takes a 6- or 7-watt bulb to replace the lamp. Do not get a night light that merely glows without a bulb. There is little reason to discontinue this step at all unless it bothers some other person. If it does, discontinue the night light after two weeks.

_____ 8. If the child objects to the removal of the night light, get a night light which merely has a glowing section. If this does not bother anybody, just leave it. If it does, discontinue it after a week or two.

At each step, praise the child for the progress being made. However, be relatively matter-of-fact and do not make a big deal of the issue. If problems arise merely move more slowly. The preparation time for bed is very important; this procedure will work much better if the child is relaxed and at ease at bedtime. Although the procedure above can take several weeks, it is easy and requires no particular preparation other than getting the equipment. If your child asks you about the changes, just tell him you are going to help him get used to less light gradually.

Final Comments

A variety of ways of handling several bedtime and sleep problems have been discussed in this chapter. If you have a problem with your child over bedtime or sleep, an approach to solving it was probably described. However, you may have a problem which was not covered, and which is causing you some concern. If this is the case, reread the chapter and see if any of the procedures described can be modified to solve your problem. For instance, the Game Board approach can be used for a wide range of things—it is merely a device for providing some occasional motivation to a child in a way which most children find fun. You can probably think up many ways to use Game Boards and many ways to apply them.

In this chapter it was stressed that most bedtime and sleep problems do not indicate any physical, medical, or general psychological problem. If the programs do not work for you, or you are convinced for various reasons that a more serious problem may exist, it is silly to keep worrying about it without checking it out. A physician, pediatrician, or psychologist may be able to help you decide. It is unlikely that you have a serious problem, but a professional may help even with a minor problem. If you do have a problem that warrants professional help, you will feel better if you do something about it rather than putting it off. And it will be reassuring to find out that your worries are groundless.

GAME CARD

You can earn one move each night by

Starting Relax Time by _____

Being in Bed by _____

GAME BOARD

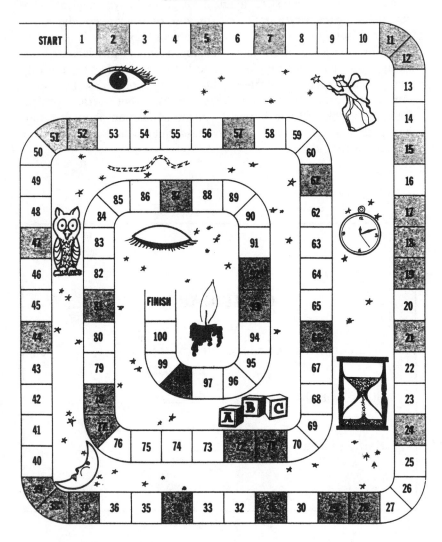

SURPRISE LIST

Daily Surprises
  1
  2
  3
  4
  5
  6
  7
  8
  9
  10
  11
  12
  13
  14
  15

Weekly Surprises
  1
  2
  3
  4
  5
  6
  7
  8
  9
  10

Twice-a-Month Surprises
  1
  2
  3
  4
  5

Use additional space if needed.

CRYING AND YELLING WORKSHEET

Date	Bedtime	Crying and Yelling Ended	Total Time
11/23	8:15	8:50 / 9:03 / 9:12 / 9:25	70

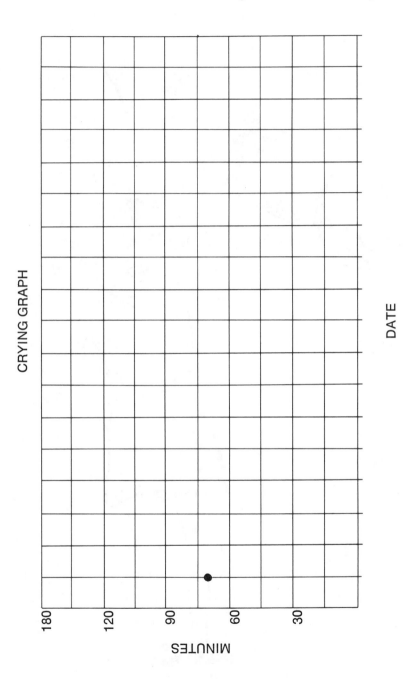

CRYING GRAPH

DATE

MINUTES

180

120

90

60

30

9.
Stop Interrupting

INTERRUPTING is an extremely annoying habit. There are few things that can make a person more angry than frequently being cut short while speaking. You get two words out of your mouth, and *bang* . . . your child is talking a mile a minute as if you hadn't said a thing.

Even though it can be a pain, interrupting isn't one of the world's most serious problems, nor is it difficult to correct. Interrupting is often the result of failing to teach good listening habits. Kids are often exuberant and tend to let this enthusiasm carry over into their speech; what they have to say seems under pressure to be said *now*. Also, adults set a poor example by interrupting children, and failing to provide a chance for them to have their say. When this is the case, interrupting is the only recourse. Sometimes we just don't point out to children that they are interrupting—or that it has a bad effect on others. Sometimes we actually encourage interrupting by listening to the interrupter, repeating what we were saying, and in general not providing any negative consequences. In this chapter we will describe a very simple and brief program which takes all of these factors into account.

How to Start

Read the entire chapter before doing anything about the problem. Try to get any other persons who talk to your child and who are concerned about the child's interrupting to read the chapter with you and then also follow the program. The program is most effective when a large part of the child's "audience" takes part in the program.

Set a good example. As you may have figured out from other chapters, the old command "Do as I say, not as I do" is ineffective with children. Children do as you do, so you have to be careful about your own actions. This means that you must not interrupt the child, nor let him or her see you interrupting others. The more children see such behavior the more likely they are to engage in it. Moreover, by not interrupting yourself you reduce the necessity for the child to interrupt you.

Put a strip of masking tape on your wrist and carry a pen with you. You are going to make a check mark on the tape each time you interrupt your child. For this practice you should define an interruption as follows:

1. Talking within less than two seconds after your child completes a sentence.
2. Talking within five seconds of a hesitation in speech which is not the end of a sentence.

If you do either of these things, place a check on your tape to indicate that you have interrupted your child.

The normal place for a person to start talking after another is when the first has completed a sentence. Yet often the first speaker has more to say than can be expressed in one sentence. If you jump right in at the end of a sentence you may interrupt the other's speech. Thus, unless you wait two seconds after a sentence it is scored as an interruption. It is also a temptation to talk when another hesitates in the middle of a sentence. Sometimes it may even be appropriate—as when someone hesitates searching for a word to express something and you provide the word for them. However, for this exercise all words or statements you make which occur within five seconds of a hesitation (not the end of a sentence) are counted as interruptions.

Keep your tape and pen with you whenever you are with your child. Record interruptions whenever you talk with the child. Draw a line each time a new conversation starts, as in the example below.

| ✓✓ | ✓✓✓ | | | ✓ ✓✓✓ | | ✓ | ✓✓✓ | | ✓

The first mark is a line indicating the start of a conversation. Two checks follow it; therefore the parent interrupted twice in that conversation. The next line shows that another conversation started, perhaps in a minute or two, perhaps several hours later. No checks follow it, so the parent did not interrupt at all in that conversation. Then another conversation started and the parent interrupted three times during that conversation. Then there were two more conversations with no parental interruptions in either. The parent interrupted three times in the next conversation. Looking back at the drawing of the tape, you will note that there were a total of nine conversations, as there are nine vertical lines. There were a total of nine interruptions, as there are nine checks. This comes out one interruption per conversation. To help you cut down on interrupting, do the following.

1. Wear the tape and carry the pen every day.
2. On the My Interrupting form at the end of the chapter, record from the tape your total interruptions (checks) and total conversations (lines) for the day. Do this every evening after your child has gone to bed.
3. Figure out the interruptions per conversation for each day and write it in the space provided on the form.
4. Continue this every day until you have three days in a row with less than one interruption per conversation.
5. Then do this every third or fourth day to make sure you are not drifting back into bad habits.

Reminding. In this step you remind your child when he or she interrupts. One problem with interrupting is that the person doing it is frequently not aware of doing it, its frequency or the way that it affects others. This section is designed to correct that.

The procedure is very simple. *Every* time your child interrupts when you are speaking, you do one of two things:

1. You state the fact. Most statements should be "You are interrupting," "I was talking," or some equivalent. Whatever statement you use, it should merely state one of these first two facts.
2. You state the effect. An example might be "I was talking, and it makes me angry to be interrupted." The nonfactual part of the statement should only mention how you feel; it should not make any statements about the child. For instance, do not say, "I was talking and it's rude to interrupt when someone else is talking." Make no statements except the factual statement plus how it makes you feel.

Do these two things alone for two days. After two days provide consequences, described in the next section.

Consequences

When your child starts to interrupt, immediately stop talking, turn around, and walk off. That's all. Do not make any comments at all. Resist the urge to wait and then repeat yourself. The minute the interruption starts, stop talking and walk off.

After you walk off you may resume talking to your child again in two or three minutes. If you want to talk to the child, just approach and start talking again as if nothing had happened. Do not explain what you did or why. If the child asks why you walked off, merely say, "You interrupted," and continue talking as if nothing had occurred. If, after you walk off, your child approaches you to talk, just start again in the same way. Be as pleasant as if nothing had happened. If you are interrupted again, repeat the consequence.

When to Use Reminders and Consequences

Anytime after you have set a good example for three days by not interrupting more than once per conversation, you can start the reminding and consequence procedures. The success of the program, and the cure for interrupting, is dependent upon your consistency. You should follow the procedures exactly and you should not stop using the procedures until the problem is solved. Here is what to do.

Days 1 and 2. On the first two days use only reminders without consequences. You remind the child every time you are interrupted. After two days your child should know what is bothering you.

Days 3 through 6. For the next four days, every time you start a new conversation with your child, remind for the first interruption; for the next, use consequences. That will end the conversation.

Days 7 and later. Starting on Day 7 and from then on, use only consequences. Every time you are interrupted, provide the consequences.

Records. No records are kept until Day 3. To make recording easy and to provide a way for you to tell when the program is working, starting on day three, mark down on the Record Form each time you provide consequences. In the column at the right add up the total times you provided consequences and thus the total interruptions for the day.

Note that this simple method of recording may mislead you as to how things are going. In Days 3 through 6 you merely provide a reminder for the first interruption in each conversation. As you do not provide consequences, you will not have a mark for the first interruption. So on Days 3 through 6 you must double the number of marks you have to obtain an accurate record.

Finishing the Program

When you feel comfortable with the reduction you have obtained in interrupting, based on your own observations and on the Record Form, discontine the consequences. However, for quite some time after this you should continue to remind your child when he or she interrupts. If interrupting increases, start the program again. Obviously, it is not realistic to assume that there will never be any interrupting. When it is low enough so that it does not seem to be a significant problem, it is reasonable to stop.

Final Comments

In this program you started by setting a good example yourself. This is a good idea for any problem; if you do not set a good example it will be much harder to get your children to behave appropriately. In the second step, reminders were used to make sure your child was aware of the problem, how it affected you, and how often it occurred. This also told the child what you expected of him or her. In the final step you provided consequences for behavior, another good general approach. In this case the consequence provided was a relatively mild and natural consequence. People tend to interrupt partly because interrupting allows them to communicate something right away. By leaving when a person interrupts, you remove the reward of communicating something immediately.

MY INTERRUPTING

Date	Interruptions (checks)	Conversations (lines)	Interruptions Conversations

RECORD FORM

Date	Consequences Tally	Total for Day
		*
		*
		*
		*

* Double tally to get the total for these days, as for each interruption with a consequence, there was one which just got a reminder.

10.
Oh, Those Chores

In all families there is work that must be done. Food must be purchased, prepared, and served. Beds must be made. Laundry must be done. Garbage must be taken care of. Rooms must be cleaned. Pets must be fed and tended to. In most families this work is shared to a greater or lesser extent. Unfortunately, getting children to do the chores often becomes the responsibility of the parents. Sometimes this is more work than doing the chores oneself.

There are many reasons for giving children chores to do. For practical reasons, it is useful for children to help get necessary jobs done. And, equally important, parents want children to help because it teaches a sense of responsibility and fairness. If there are benefits in having children do chores, there are also benefits in having children do them without constant reminders, nagging, and arguments. Arguments of this sort can sometimes become so common that they color other aspects of parent-child relationships. This chapter presents a program for teaching children to do their chores without being nagged.

How to Start

Read the chapter through from the beginning to the end before starting the program. Go over both the program and the illustration carefully and make sure you understand how the illustration fits the program. Then come back to the beginning and start the program.

If you are having difficulty getting your child to do several jobs it is best to use the program on only one set of chores at a time. When the child's behavior is satisfactory in one area, repeat the entire program for the second set of chores. Start the program first for the most important problem. After that is solved, start all over again on the next one.

Some other chapters in this book cover problems which can rightly be called chores—keeping a room clean, for example. Check the table of contents to see if there is a specific program that might be more appropriate for the chore that needs doing.

Do You Have a Problem?

There is no rule to tell you when you actually have a problem. If you think you have a problem, you probably do. To help decide what you can reasonably expect children to do, we have included an Evaluation Sheet at the end of this chapter. The Evaluation Sheet is designed to assess the situation with one child for one set of chores. Should you want more than one, make a copy of the sheet.

Look at the sample, which describes Sam's job of caring for the dog for a five-day period. In the first column the job is broken down into its major components. Three components were necessary to describe Sam's dog-care chores. A relatively simple criterion for each—the standards for a satisfactory job—was then listed in the second column. In the third column the days and the times when these jobs must be done were listed. Sam was then rated on this job for five days as follows:

0: Did not do at all
1: Did a little of job
2: Did most but not all of job
3: Did all of job
X: No opportunity or need to do job

On four out of five days Sam fed the dog and received ratings of 3. On one day he did not feed the dog and received a rating of 0. It was decided that for this component Sam would get either a 3 or a 0, with no in-between scores. On three days Sam took the dog out the required number of times and received three ratings. On the third day Sam forgot to take the dog out after school but did the other times, so he received a 2. On the last day Sam took the dog out only in the morning before school. For this he received a rating of 1. There were only two days during the period on which the dog had accidents. On Day 3 when this occurred Sam cleaned up perfectly, but on Day 5 he did not clean up until twenty-five minutes after the accident was reported. It was decided that this deserved a rating of 2.

Based upon this evaluation it was decided that Sam did a fairly good job with his chores related to the dog but needed to become a bit more consistent.

You may have problems with several chores. It is not always easy to decide how many different chores exist. Chores that are not closely related or similar should be treated as separate chores. For instance, "helping keep the house clean" is probably too general. For one child this might be broken down into three chores:

- Keeping your room clean
- Helping with Saturday housecleaning
- Putting things away in the hall

Each of these is a group of related tasks that occur either in the same place or all at the same time. Each would be treated as a separate chore and worked on one at a time. After you have broken your problem down into specific chores, pick the one which bothers you most as the one on which to begin. This is the chore you will evaluate. Write it on the top of the Evaluation Sheet.

The second task in determining if you have a problem is to decide on and list the components which make up this chore. Each component should be a clearly separate task, that is, a job performed all at the same time which can be judged easily as either done or not done.

After you have listed the components, list the criteria for each. By these criteria you will decide if the component has been satisfactorily completed. If you cannot write clear criteria for a component, you probably need to break the task down into more than one component.

Then write down when each component should be done. Some, such as cleaning up accidents (in the illustration), may not have set times; when they should be done will depend upon circumstances which cannot be predicted. However, in such cases write the circumstances and some time down as clearly as possible.

The final job before starting the evaluation is to decide on the rating values. A rating sheet is provided. You will note that the standards for 0 and for 3 ratings are already filled in; 0 is obtained if the component is not done at all, 3 is obtained if it is done completely. A 1 is obtained when only a small part of a job is done. A 2 is given when most but not all of the job is done. Write down some notes for 1 and 2 ratings which are sufficient to make your ratings fairly consistent. Some jobs are most convenient to rate as either done (3) or not done (0) with no in-between ratings.

The next task is obvious: Do the ratings for five days. However, omit days which are atypical—when your child is ill or out of town, for example.

The last task is to look at your ratings and decide if you have a problem. Most people would probably think that ratings which average close to 1 are a problem and that ratings that average close to 2 indicate only a trivial problem. However, you must decide.

Improving Things

If you decide that you do have a problem, the approach is simple. The first step is to state clearly exactly what you want done. This will also include explaining why this needs to be done and providing a chance for your child to make suggestions for changes. The next is to plan a series of steps to teach your child gradually to do the entire chore in a reliable manner. The third step is to decide upon consequences which will reward satisfactory performances and deny reward when the task is not done properly. After all this, start the program.

Rationale form. At the end of the chapter is the Rationale form and a sample filled out for Sam's jobs. In the first column, "Components," merely indicate which part of the chore you are talking about. In the second column, indicate honest reasons why this job has to be done at all. In the third column, indicate why it should be done meeting the standards you have described in the criteria column of the Evaluation Sheet, and in the fourth column, why it needs to be done at or by a certain time. In the last column give the reasons why the particular child in question, rather than someone else, should do it. Look at the sample for Sam to see how this can be done.

By completing such a Rationale form you make clear why your expectations are reasonable rather than arbitrary. Obviously, there are going to be differences of opinion on all of these items. However, even if there are disagreements, this form shows you are being fair, and not authoritarian.

Fill out the Rationale form for the chore you are going to work on first. Make sure that you put the child's name in the heading for the last column. Use pencil.

Now go over this form with your child. Explain the task for each component. Then for each component explain the reasons that the task needs to be done, the criteria, the time limits, and the reasons why you feel the child in question should do this task. If there are disagreements, they should be worked out. This may take some time, but if your reasons are valid you should be able to communicate them. If your child raises an objection which you feel is reasonable, feel free to change things. When agreement is reached, you and the child should initial the form in the top right corner.

Approximating perfection. In the best of all possible worlds everybody would do everything perfectly from the very beginning. In the real world, we know, this isn't the case—and particularly not with children's chores.

If your child received ratings below 3 on the Evaluation Sheet it may be unreasonable to expect perfect performance right away. Instead of requiring perfection from the beginning and then exposing yourself and the child to failure, this program suggests temporarily lowering your expectations. Requirements are then regularly and systematically raised until the chore is completely done regularly.

There are three ways to do this:

1. In the beginning you can require that the child complete certain, but not all, of the components of the chore. This approach is best when the chore contains a large number of very simple components, some of which can be initially omitted. For instance, if the chore is taking care of the yard and some of the components are raking, weeding, trimming hedges, cutting bushes, spraying, fertilizing, watering, etc., this might be appropriate. Some of these tasks could be omitted at first.

2. In the beginning do not require that all the criteria be met, but leave all components in. This is best for a chore for which each task has several criteria to be met and it is easy to omit some of them at first. Suppose the chore is care of the family car. The components might be (1) washing the car, (2) keeping the car filled with gas, oil, water, air in the tires, brake fluid, etc., and (3) listing repairs and taking the car for a lube job and for all repairs every two months. The first component (washing the car) might include (a) removing tar, (b) using chrome cleaner on chrome, (3) vacuuming the inside, (d) using upholstery cleaner on dash and seats, (e) washing the outside, and (f) waxing the outside. In the initial stages you might require only washing the outside and vacuuming the inside, omitting the other criteria for a washed car.

3. In the beginning you may not require that the chore be done

as often as you will later. For instance, suppose the chore is dusting, straightening, and vacuuming the family room. Eventually you might want each of these done twice a week. To start you might set up a schedule requiring that they be done every ten days. This procedure is good for a chore whose frequency can reasonably be reduced.

Look over the chore you are starting on and decide which of the three types of approximations seems easiest to use with this chore.

Your next task is to reduce the chore to a reasonable starting approximation. To do this, work with your Evaluation Sheet and the Initial Task Sheet at the end of the chapter. On the Initial Task Sheet write a first approximation to the final description of the chore given on the Evalution Form. Reduce the final task by either omitting components, reducing criteria, or cutting down the times listed on the Evaluation Sheet until the chore description is approximately half that on the Evaluation Sheet. Then copy this initial task requirement on to the Initial Task Sheet. Fill in the components, the criteria, and the "When" column, but leave the last column blank for now.

Now that you have done this, fill in the Middle Task Sheet in the same manner. However, on this sheet add more components, criteria, or times so that the middle sheet requires about three-quarters of the final chore rather than half. Then copy the components, criteria, and "When" section from the Evaluation Sheet onto the Final Task Sheet. Thus the Initial Task Sheet, the Middle Task Sheet, and the Final Task Sheet are three steps in completing the entire chore. The Initial sheet has about half the task required, the Middle sheet has about three-quarters of the task required, and the Final sheet has the entire task required.

Consequences

There are three topics to cover under providing consequences. The first is determining the number of points earned by doing chores. The second is deciding what the points can be traded for. The last is going over the correct use of praise and approval for chores.

Points. Each component of the chore should be assigned a point value. Don't worry about the exact number of points; if it turns out to be wrong, it will be easy to correct.

Look at the Initial Point Planning Sheet at the end of the chapter. On the left is a column for "Components." These are the same as those listed on your Initial Task Sheet. In the next column, "Times per Week," list the number of times each component of the chore needs to be done per week. If a component may be done less than once per week, list a 1. The next column is called "Value per Time," and in it you will rate how important and difficult doing that component just once is, regardless of whether the task must be done once a week, once a day, or once a month. Rate it 1 (low) to 5 (high). In the last column ("Total Points") you will put down the total that can be earned for each component in one week—the product of the times per week multiplied by the point value.

At the bottom of the "Total Points" column is a box in which to write the maximum points. These are found by adding up the total points for each component of your chore. This is the maximum number of points which can be earned in a week if all components on the Initial Task Sheet are completed satisfactorily.

Copy the points per time from the Point Planning Sheet to the "Points per Time" column on the Initial Task Sheet.

Using the two remaining Point Planning Sheets decide on points for the Middle and Final Task Sheets in a similar manner. However, remember that more components, tasks, or times are required in these programs. So give fewer points for each instance of a component, until you can get the total points on each of these sheets to come out approximately the same as for the initial sheet. If it is hard to get them very close to the same total, it would be better to have slightly more than slightly less.

Point trade-ins. The next task is to decide upon rewards which can be earned with points. You may make something the child is now getting "free," such as allowance, dependent upon the points. Or you may think up some entirely new reward. In either case, use something that you are sure will be desirable to the child. You may use a combination of things. Procedures to help you decide on a reward or rewards (if you do not already have something in mind) are described in Chapter 1 and elsewhere.

The method of figuring out how much each reward is worth in points is very simple. Get the Reward Sheet from the end of the chapter. In the labeled space provided copy the maximum points possible to earn in the initial stage of this program from the Initial Point Planning Sheet.

Now list the rewards you have decided to provide. Space is provided for up to eight rewards, but you may not have this many.

Now decide on the number of points required to earn each reward.

Start with the first reward. Pretend that your child is going to earn the maximum points possible. Also pretend that your child is going to spend all of those points of the first reward. Let's say the first reward is extra money. Suppose that the maximum points your child can earn is about 40. How much money do you feel it is reasonable for your child to earn if this is the only reward selected? If you feel 40¢ a week is the most, for Reward Number 1 write "1¢ per pt." If you feel it is reasonable for your child to earn a maximum of $1.20 per week on the program (if that were the only reward taken) write "3¢ per pt." Thus if your child earned all 40 points and each was worth 3¢, the child would earn the $1.20.

Now list the second reward and pretend that is the only reward which will be selected. Suppose the second reward is a trip to town. If you feel that a trip every other week is a reasonable maximum for doing all the tasks, you would write "80 pts." At 40 pts. per week maximum your child would have to earn the maximum points for two weeks to get a trip. Now list the next reward and figure it the same way.

Do not worry about being exact, since you do not know the exact number of points your child will actually earn. Later on we will discuss changing these point values if they seem too easy or too hard.

You may need to list a few special rules at the bottom of the Reward Sheet. For instance, if staying up late is a reward you may want to limit the time or the days on which the privilege can be bought. Add whatever rules you feel are needed to make this plan workable.

Each time your child completes any component or daily part of a component of a chore, mark the points down on the Bank Balance. You can tell how many points any work is worth by looking at the "Points per Time" column of the Point Planning Sheet. Your child should be able to spend points as soon as they are earned if this is possible. Obviously you may not be able to provide a trip or something you need to buy the instant the child earns enough points, but you should try to do this as soon as possible. As soon as a reward is delivered, write down the number of points it cost in the "Spent" column. Every time points are earned or spent, mark down the new balance in the "Balance" column. Put each transaction on a separate line even if there are several a day. Thus, each time points are earned or spent you will fill in the date, and keep track of points earned and spent.

Praise and approval. Always give praise and approval when your child completes any aspect of a chore correctly. If you remember, you might also say how many points that earned. When a task is not done, ignore it.

Posting. Post the following on a bulletin board or wall:

Initial Task Sheet

Reward Sheet

Bank Balance

Whenever you have a question about points earned, or need to determine the cost of a reward or to enter something on the Bank Balance, you will come here.

Summary

There have been a lot of forms and procedures for you to follow. These probably seemed more complicated than they actually are. The steps are summarized below:

1. You filled out an Evaluation Form for the chore you wish to start with. You made sure this is the chore that bothers you most and that it should not be broken down into several separate chores.
   a. You listed the separate components or tasks that made up this chore.
   b. For each component you listed the criteria that tell whether that component is done correctly.
   c. You listed the days of the week and times that each component should be done.
2. You rated your child on a 0-3 scale for five days for each component of this chore. You then made a final decision as to whether this is a problem.
3. You filled out a Rationale Sheet. On this you listed each component by number, using the same numbers as on the Evaluation Form. You then gave the reasons why the chore needs to be done at all, why it must be done in a certain way, why it must be done at certain times, and why your child should do it.
4. You filled out an Initial, Middle, and Final Task Sheet. The Final Task Sheet was basically the same as the Evaluation Form as far as components, criteria and "when." The Middle Task Sheet was a simpler, cut-down approximation to the Final

Task Sheet, and the Initial Task Sheet was still easier and simpler.

5. Using the Point Planning Sheet, you figured out how many times per week each component on the Initial Task Sheet needed to be performed, how many points to give for each performance, the total points that each component could earn per week, and the total maximum points that could be earned according to the tasks on the Initial Task Sheet. You then did the same for the Middle and Final Task Sheets, trying to keep the total number of maximum points approximately the same on all three sheets.

6. You then figured out a list of possible rewards and how many points each reward would cost. You listed these on the Reward Sheet along with any rules you felt were necessary.

7. You went over the Bank Balance Sheet.

8. You posted the Initial Task Sheet, the Reward Sheet, and the Bank Balance Sheet.

Explaining and Starting

Show your child the three posted forms. Go over the tasks on the Initial Task Sheet. Explain exactly what each task is, how it is to be done, and when it must be done. Then, from the last column, tell how many points can be earned each time your child performs a task.

Then explain the Reward Sheet. Explain the details of earning and spending points, and that you may have to change the cost of rewards. Then explain how the Bank Balance will be used to keep a record.

To make sure that your child understands all this, have the child explain it to you. Correct any errors or misconceptions.

Problems

There are several problems which may arise. Here are the most common and what'to do about them.

1. Child does not earn enough points for rewards. (Lower the cost of rewards.)

2. Child earns too many points. (Raise the cost of rewards.)

3. Child earns points but does not spend them. (Discuss adding new rewards with the child. If the child has better ideas which are acceptable to you, add them, giving them values as you did for the original rewards.)

Progressing

When your child has done a pretty good job on the tasks listed on the Initial Task Sheet for about five days, it may be time to change. Your child is doing a good job if he or she is earning nearly all the points possible and you are not having any of the problems listed in the prior section. When this happens get the Middle Task Sheet out. Tell your child that you are changing the program slightly and go over the differences between the Initial and Middle Task Sheets. Then remove the Initial Task Sheet and post the Middle Task Sheet. In the same way, switch to the Final Task Sheet after five good days on the Middle Task Sheet. Treat problems which develop as described in the prior section.

Ending. When things have gone well on the Final Task Sheet for at least two weeks tell your child that things are going so well you are going to discontinue the program. Remove the Reward Sheet and the Bank Balance Sheet. Continue to give rewards in an informal manner without recording points when you feel jobs are done well. Leave the Task Sheet posted as a reminder.

Adding a program for another chore. If you are having a problem with another chore, *after* ending the program for the first chore start one for the second chore in the same manner. Continue to give occasional informal rewards for good performance on the first chore along with the rewards given for the second chore. Following this program conscienciously should help eliminate problems with chores.

EVALUATION SHEET

CHORE____ Daily care of dog   PERFORMER____ Sam

Components	Criteria	When	Ratings: Day				
			1	2	3	4	5
1 Give fresh food and water	Bowls full when leaves for school	7 days a week by 8:30 a.m.	3	3	3	0	3
2 Take dog out	Dog taken out of house into back yard	7 days a week, once in a.m., once in p.m., once after dinner	3	3	2	3	1
3 Clean up "accidents" by dog	Waste removed, floor or carpet cleaned	Within 15 minutes after noticed	x	x	3	x	2
4							
5							
6							

EVALUATION SHEET

CHORE _____   PERFORMER _____

Components	Criteria	When	Ratings: Day				
			1	2	3	4	5
1							
2							
3							
4							
5							
6							

THE GOOD KID BOOK

RATING SHEET

Component	To get a rating of			
	0	1	2	3
1	none			all
2	none			all
3	none			all
4	none			all
5	none			all
6	none			all

RATIONALE

Component	Why Needs to Be Done	Why Should Meet Criteria	Why Done That Time	Why Sam Should Do It
1.	Dog will starve, dog will chew other things if no food. Dog will dehydrate or drink from toilet. Dog will bark with no food, etc.	Finishes this much in a day. Needs full bowl to last.	Eats what's left at night so no food by morning.	Dad and Mom leave early and do not have time. Mary cleans up breakfast.
2.	Dog will go in house if not taken out.	Yard is best place to go in terms of mess, and in terms of safety; i.e., safer than front with street.	If does not go out this often will go in house. Can't wait longer at these times.	Mom and Dad not home many of these times—they are already working. Mary has to do shopping so already has work.
3.	Stains carpets and floors, unsanitary, also not pleasing.	If both not done does not solve problems in 1st column.	If left longer stains and smell difficult or impossible to remove.	Dog only does this if not taken out, and this is Sam's job.

RATIONALE

Component	Why Needs to Be Done	Why Should Meet Criteria	Why Done That Time	Why ____ Should Do It
1.				
2.				
3.				

INITIAL TASK SHEET

CHORE_____   PERFORMER_____

Components	Criteria	When	Points per Time
1.			
2.			
3.			
4.			
5.			
6.			

MIDDLE TASK SHEET

CHORE _____

PERFORMER _____

Components	Criteria	When	Points per Time
1.			
2.			
3.			
4.			
5.			
6.			

FINAL TASK SHEET

CHORE _____   PERFORMER _____

Components	Criteria	When	Points per Time
1.			
2.			
3.			
4.			
5.			
6.			

THE GOOD KID BOOK

POINT PLANNING SHEET

INITIAL

Component	Times per Week	Points per Time	Total Points
1.			
2.			
3.			
4.			
5.			
6.			

MAXIMUM POINTS_____

POINT PLANNING SHEET

MIDDLE

Component	Times per Week	Points per Time	Total Points
1.			
2.			
3.			
4.			
5.			
6.			

MAXIMUM POINTS_____

THE GOOD KID BOOK

POINT PLANNING SHEET

FINAL

Component	Times per Week	Points per Time	Total Points
1.			
2.			
3.			
4.			
5.			
6.			

MAXIMUM POINTS_____

REWARD SHEET

		Points
	Maximum Points	

Rewards

1	
2	
3	
4	
5	
6	
7	
8	

RULES:

THE GOOD KID BOOK

BANK BALANCE

Date	Earned	Spent	Balance

11.
What About Bedwetting?

CHILDREN stop wetting their beds at different ages. Most children become dry between ages two and three; some before the age of two. Many children continue to wet the bed until about age three and a half or four, and then learn to remain dry without difficulty. About 15% of five-year-olds are regular bedwetters. Bedwetting (which is technically called "enuresis") beyond these ages is more common in boys than in girls—about 80% of continued bedwetters are boys. Bedwetting in adolescents and adults is probably more common than most people believe.

Many experts, physicians, and parents believe that protracted bedwetting is a symptom of some underlying emotional problem, yet there is no evidence which proves this. Most probably bedwetting is due to a simple learning failure. However, it is obvious that a child who continues to wet the bed at an age when his brothers, sisters, and friends are dry may become upset. He may do things to hide it and avoid embarrassment, he may be teased or bothered by parents, and his activities may be restricted. For instance, a child who wets may avoid sleeping away from home or become upset over nap times at school. However, this is a result of bedwetting, not the cause of it.

Some parents and physicians believe that surgery can correct bedwetting. There are a few rare and unusual anatomic disorders that can be corrected by surgery; in other cases this is not successful.

Many experts have suggested restricting liquids for a bedwetter for several hours before bedtime. Undoubtedly, a child with less urine to void will wet the bed less. However, as the child learns nothing new, when the child does have to go the child will be as likely to wet the bed as ever. In addition, restriction of liquids may decrease the child's bladder capacity and make bedwetting even worse in the long run. Finally, restriction of liquids gives the child less opportunity to learn bladder control, so the bedwetting may persist for a longer time.

There are nonmedical approaches which work well to correct bedwetting. We will discuss several and point out the good and bad points of each so that you can choose among them.

In selecting a program or approaches to use, it does not matter if the child has always been a bedwetter, or was dry for some time and then started wetting the bed again. However, if an older child starts wetting the bed it is always wise to have a medical exam. If no problems are found, just start one of the programs in this chapter. With any child under age five who wets the bed it is wise to have a medical exam to rule out the possibility of a medical problem.

How to Start

Your child is not wetting the bed because of some hopeless neurosis. Nor is the child wetting the bed to "get at" you or because of some failure as a parent on your part. The child is wetting the bed because he—or more rarely, she—has not learned to stay dry. Considering what we know about the physiology of retaining urine until awaking, it is more surprising that most children learn to stay dry than that some do not.

Never criticize, punish, or embarrass your child for bedwetting. You should tell your child that it is time to learn how to stay dry at night, and that you will help. Make it clear that it may take a while, but you are sure your child can do it. Stress that you will show the child how to learn to stay dry. Ignore failures, praise successes, and have patience.

Read all the approaches to bedwetting which are described in this chapter. Decide which ones you feel are most appropriate. Then start the training following the program outlines.

Liquids. No matter what approach you use to correct bedwetting, you should not restrict the child's intake of liquids. As a matter of fact, you should do just the opposite. Retaining urine enlarges the bladder, and a child with a large bladder will be better able to retain liquids than a child with a small bladder. In addition, it is important to give the learner as much practice as you can. So in all effective approaches to bedwetting you give the child a lot of liquids, both during the day and in the evening. Of course, this will make for more bedwetting at the start, but it will also help your child to retain urine

better, and to learn to control bedwetting in less time. The first step for every approach is lots of liquids, particularly in the evening.

Preparation, practice, and pretest. Certain skills which are not directly related to retaining urine until awaking are essential if a child is going to stay dry at night. These consists of the following:

1. Being able to find the bathroom.
2. Being able to turn on the light in the bathroom, if necessary.
3. Being able to take down, take off, or open bedclothes to go to the bathroom.
4. Being able to get back in bed.

You cannot assume that a child can do these things, even though he or she may do all or some of them during the day. To remain dry at night the child must have practice in these routines.

Before starting the alarm program or one of the waking programs, go through the following preparation.

1. Tell your child that at bedtime for a few nights you are going to give some practice in going to the bathroom at night.
2. Put the child in bed after dark. Turn off all lights in the house which are not on all night.
3. Tell the child to get out of bed and go to the bathroom, and to pretend that he or she is urinating (use the child's term for this). To do it correctly, the child must go into the bathroom, turn on whatever lights are necessary, and get in the proper position for urination. The child must then go through this procedure correctly in reverse, ending up back in bed with the lights out. No adult help should be given.
4. If the child cannot do this routine correctly with no errors and no help on the first night you request it, you must teach it to the child—otherwise the bedwetting won't stop. To teach the procedure, instruct the child in exactly what to do for each step, then demonstrate it, then help the child to do it, then have the child do it alone. Praise the child for trying, and for correct responses at each step.
5. After the child does it correctly once, have the child do it four more times.
6. Have the child do this until for three nights in a row the child can do it absolutely correctly with no help, reminders, or cues —except being told to pretend that he or she is going to urinate. Continue doing this five times a night until the child is 100% perfect on all five tries with no help, on three nights in a row.

Bladder Training

Bladder training is an approach that stretches the size of your child's bladder, and thus makes it easier for the child to retain more urine for a longer time. Sometimes it solves bedwetting all by itself, but in most cases it is a useful additional procedure along with other techniques. If it doesn't work alone, just add one of the more specific approaches. The bladder training will help speed up any other technique you use, so it is probably worth trying for two or three weeks first. If it works, great. If it does not, you have not wasted time, but provided a good background for further efforts.

Program description. The concept on which this program is based is very simple. If, when a child has to go, the child waits a *short* period of time before going, the child will get practice in retaining urine. In addition, by learning to go less often the child will retain more urine and will increase bladder capacity. Each time the child has to go to the bathroom, he or she waits a few minutes. In the beginning, this waiting period is made very brief so every child can succeed. Based upon the child's successful efforts, this amount of time is gradually increased, improving the ability to retain urine and increasing bladder capacity. In 33% to 45% of children with bedwetting problems this procedure alone has been reported to correct the problem. In those for whom this technique does not correct the problem, additional and slightly more complex procedures are appropriate. Even when this simple procedure alone does not "cure" bedwetting, it should make other approaches easier to carry out.

How to use it. There are two ways you can use this program, depending upon how impatient you are to solve the problem.

If you are very impatient, start this program and at the same time also start one of the waking programs or the alarm program described later in this chapter. This is slightly more work, but is also more likely to be successful on the first try.

If you are not impatient you can start this program alone for several weeks. It is very little work. If it is successful, well and good. If it is not, then start either a waking program or the alarm program.

After you have read this entire chapter, come back to this point and decide which you are going to do.

As for all programs, the child should drink a lot of liquids.

Step 1—explaining. Tell your child that you are going to start a simple, easy game which may help him or her learn to stay dry at night. Say that the game involves three parts.

1. Whenever you and the child are home and awake, and the child has to go to the bathroom, the child should come tell you before going.
2. When the child tells you, you will ask the child to wait for a little while. If the child can hold it for this short time, he or she will get a small reward. If the child cannot hold it but must go immediately there will be no reward.
3. If the child succeeds in waiting you will then give the reward.

Step 2—rewards. Decide upon rewards. These do not have to be the same every time. A small glass of juice, a cookie, a candy, letting the child play with some favorite toy, your playing with the child for two or three minutes—any small thing will do. However, prepare some rewards in advance.

Step 3—praise. There are two situations in which you always praise and compliment your child.

1. When the child comes and tells you that he or she has to go instead of just going without telling you, give praise. Thank the child for telling you. If the child goes without telling you, ignore it.
2. After the child tells you he or she has to go, you will tell the child to wait a little bit (explained later). If the child waits before going, you praise the child again, and then give the reward. If the child cannot wait until the time is up, just make a matter-of-fact comment like "that's OK." Do not praise the child or give a reward.

Step 4—first waiting period. Start with a five-minute waiting period. Thus, when your child comes and tells you he or she has to go, look at your watch or a clock and see what time it is. Then say, "See if you can wait a little bit of time. I'll tell you when it is up." When five minutes are up, say, "OK, time's up, time to go."

If the first four times you try this your child cannot wait five minutes, reduce the waiting time to three minutes. If your child still cannot wait this long, reduce it to a minute.

Step 5—increasing the waiting period. When your child succeeds in waiting for the required time two days in a row, increase the time by two minutes. For example, if you started with a one-minute waiting period, you will now increase it to three minutes.

Your child is successful when these two things happen:

1. The child tells you he or she has to go nearly every time the child urinates during the day at home.
2. The child is able to wait the time limit nearly every time. One or two exceptions are OK. With three or more do not call the day successful.

Step 6—failures. If, when you increase the waiting period, your child is unsuccessful half the time or more, decrease the waiting period by one minute. The waiting time should be increased when the child succeeds, as described in Step 5.

Step 7—further increases. If your child is successful with the new waiting period for three days, increase it by two minutes again. Then, if he or she is successful with the new waiting period, increase it again by two minutes. Keep doing this until you reach a thirty-minute waiting period. This is the longest waiting period you will use. Treat failures as in Step 6.

Step 8—starting and stopping. This step is designed to increase the amount of control the child has over retaining or stopping the flow of urine. It should be carried out twice a day after the child has waited for the waiting period and is about to go urinate. Go into the bathroom with the child. Tell the child to start urinating (use the child's word). Two seconds after you hear the flow of urine, tell the child to stop, and "hold it" for a few seconds. After five seconds, tell the child to go again. Again, after two seconds, have the child hold it for five seconds. Continue until the child has no more urine to void. Do this twice a day throughout the program.

Step 9—bedchecks. When you reach a thirty-minute waiting period, start checking the child's bed every morning to see if he or she stayed dry all night. If you are also using a waking program you may already be doing this. If not, start now.

Step 10—stopping. The way you end this program depends upon whether or not you are also using a waking program or the alarm program, and the results you obtain.

If you are using another program continue this program with a thirty-minute waiting period until you stop the other program. The other programs have instructions for stopping.

If you are using bladder training alone, continue bedchecks for three weeks. If there is a lot of improvement (child only wets the bed about half as much as before the program), continue the program until you have had at least two successful weeks with no bedwetting. If bedwetting starts again, just start the program again, using the thirty-minute waiting period. Follow all the usual procedures starting at this point.

If there is not major improvement, but there is a bit, continue the program but also start a waking program or the alarm program.

If there is no improvement, stop the program and start the alarm program or one of the waking programs alone.

Records. To help you keep track of the program a record-keeping form is included at the end of the chapter. Use it as follows.

1. *Date.* Fill in the date at the start of each day. The rest of the space in that horizontal row will be for your records that day.
2. *Waiting time.* Fill in that day's waiting time when you fill in the date. Steps 4 through 7 tell you how to figure the waiting time.
3. *No notification.* If you notice that your child is going to the bathroom to urinate without telling you and then waiting, make an X in the "No Notification" box. Make an X each time you notice this. Do not spy, quiz, or check up on your child, just note those you happen to catch. This will help you decide if your child is successful (Step 5).
4. *Waited.* Each time your child comes and tells you he or she has to go, and then waits the full waiting time before going, put an X in the "waited" box.
5. *Didn't Wait.* If your child cannot last out the waiting time, put an X in the "Didn't Wait" box. Make an X everytime this occurs during the day.
6. *Wet bed.* After you reach the thirty-minute waiting period, check the bed each morning. If it indicates the child wet during the night, make an X in the "Wet Bed" box.
7. *Dry bed.* Make an X in the "Dry Bed" box when bedchecks indicate the child did not wet during the night.

Regular Waking Program

This waking program is designed for the child who wets the bed fairly frequently, say three or more times per week. It requires an alarm clock, pencil and paper, and parents who are willing to get up quite often during the night. As the program progresses, parents have to get up less and less, until it is not necessary to get up at all. Read the entire program before starting.

Step 1—assessment. This is by far the hardest part of this program. Fortunately, it only lasts five nights. It is best if you carry out this assessment on five consecutive nights. If you cannot, try to do it on five nights as close together as possible.

For five nights, set an alarm and check your child every hour, starting when the child goes to bed, and ending one hour before the child wakes up. Feel your child's bed to see if the child has wet. You do not have to wake the child. On the Assessment form at the end of this chapter mark whether the bed was wet or dry. Also mark down the time the child went to bed. Once the bed is wet, you do not have to check any further that night.

In addition, give the child lots of liquids in the evening before bed. So you do the following: (1) give liquids in the evening, (2) using an alarm clock or kitchen timer check the child's bed to see if it is wet every hour from when the child goes to bed until morning, except (3) once the bed is wet you do not have to check further. Finally, you (4) record your results on the Assessment form.

Step 2—Start Time. On the Assessment form calculate the amount of time from when the child went to bed until the bed was wet when you checked, for each of the five days. Then find the smallest of these times. In other words, what was the shortest time in the five days between when the child went to bed and you first found a wet bed? This is the Start Time.

If you wake the child within the Start Time, the bed will probably still be dry.

Step 3—Waking Interval. If the Start Time is three or more hours, the Waking Interval is the same as the Start Time. If the Start Time is one or two hours, the Waking Interval is two hours.

Step 4—Beginning Program. This is the next-hardest part of this program. As you will see, as the program progresses you have to get up less and less. At this stage each evening you do the following:

1. You have already figured out the Start Time and the Waking Interval. Write these on the Beginning Program form. You only have to do this on the first day. The rest you do every night.
2. Give the child liquids in the evening.
3. Put the child to bed whenever you wish, and write the bedtime down on the Beginning Program form.
4. Write down the first time you will have to wake the child that night in the box provided. This time is one Start Time after bedtime.
5. Write down the rest of the times you have to wake the child that night. Each of these times is one waking interval after the time before.

6. Set an alarm or timer so it will ring at the first time.
7. When the alarm rings, wake the child. Make the child go to the bathroom and urinate. The child must get out of bed without help and walk unaided to the bathroom. You must not carry the child. Shake the child awake and say, "Time to go to the bathroom." Let the child do the rest without help.
8. If the child was wet, circle the time on the form. If the child was not wet, do not circle the time.
9. If the child was wet, make the child change to clean bedclothes. The child must do as much of this without help as the child can do at bedtime. Then change the bedding. The child should do as much of this without help as the child could do during the day. Then thank the child and put the child to bed again.
10. If the child was dry, merely thank the child and put him or her to bed again after the trip to the bathroom.
11. Set the alarm for the next time you have to get the child up. When it rings, repeat the entire procedure.
12. The last time you wake the child before morning, check your record and see if the child was dry all night (no times circled). If the child was, post the Perfect Star (at the end of the chapter) in the child's room. Put a candy, sweet roll, or some favorite juice or dry cereal beside the child's bed where the child can find it in the morning. With an older child you can omit the reward if you feel it is inappropriate.

Continue this exact procedure until your child is dry the first time you wake him or her for five times in a row.

Step 5—Second Program. This program is exactly like the Beginning Program except you start waking the child later in the evening. The New Start Time is the original Start Time plus one Waking Interval. As you start later, you will also have to wake the child one time fewer during the night. Use the Second Program form. Do everything else exactly the same as you did in the Beginning Program.

Continue this exact procedure until your child is dry the first time you wake him or her for five times in a row.

Step 6—later programs. You continue this procedure through the Third, Fourth, Fifth, and Sixth Program until your child is dry for the entire night. On each program, each time your child is dry on the first awakening for five times in a row, you move to the next program. Each program is the same, except the New Start Time is increased by one Waking Interval over the last one. Just keep this up until your child is dry all night. With each new program, you have to get up one less time per night. If your child sleeps less than twelve hours a night you will not have to go through all six programs. Forms are provided.

Step 7—relapses. It is unlikely that progress through these programs will be perfectly smooth, with no relapses. If your child is not dry on the first time for an entire week, go back to the previous program. Other than this, ignore relapses.

Step 8—absolute failure. If you are having no luck at all, go over the program carefully and make sure you are following it exactly. You cannot determine if the program is a failure unless you have tried it for three to four weeks. However, in the unlikely event of complete failure, change to the alarm program, described later.

Step 9—finishing. After you have completed the last program you no longer need to wake your child at night. However, for at least three or four weeks you should check the child's bed each morning. If the child is dry, continue to post the star, and give a reward then.

Once you get the swing of this approach, it is easy to carry out and easy to understand. You can help it along by praising your child when things are going well, ignoring bad nights, and otherwise being positive about the whole thing. The program is obviously easier if two adults alternate getting up or share the chore in some other way. However, by the third program you will have to get up only three or four times a night, depending upon how long your child sleeps and the Start Time and Waking intervals you started with.

Variable Waking Program

This waking program can be used with any bedwetter. However, unlike the previous program it is somewhat more suitable for the child who wets with no regular pattern or who wets the bed less than three times per week. Like the Regular Waking Program it requires an alarm clock, pencil, paper, and a parent willing to get up several times per night for a while. It is also like the previous program in that as it progresses, the parent has to get up less and less.

Overview. Six schedules are provided. These schedules indicate how long after bedtime you are to wake the child and take the child to the bathroom. The first schedule requires waking the child six times per night, and the last requires waking the child once per night. If your child sleeps less than twelve hours a night you may not have to wake the child this often. The times selected to wake the child are arbitrary and vary each night. For reasons that are not clear there is some evidence that children awakened at random times develop nighttime bladder control better than those awakened on a fixed schedule.

Schedules. Each schedule lists the day on the left. After each day, there is a space where you write in the time the child goes to bed. The numbers following the bedtime indicate hours after bedtime. Look at Schedule 1, Day 1. There is an X under Hour 1. This means that one hour after bedtime you will wake the child. There is also an X under Hour 2. This means that you would wake the child again two hours after bedtime. The next X indicates that you would wake the child again four hours after bedtime. You continue this until the child gets up in the morning, at which point you skip the rest of the Xs.

Using the schedules. The schedules are rather simple to use, even though getting up may not be. Whichever schedule you are using, start with Day 1, then Day 2, and so on. If you run out of days before moving to a new schedule, just start over with Day 1. How you determine which schedule to use, and when to move on, will be explained later. To start, give the child liquids in the evening, and put the child to bed at the usual time. You then record the bedtime hour, and set the alarm for the first time you will wake the child.

Waking procedure. After you record the bedtime and set the alarm, follow these steps.

1. When the alarm rings, wake the child. Make the child go to the bathroom and urinate. The child must get out of bed and walk to the bathroom unaided. You must not carry the child. Shake the child awake and say, "Time to go to the bathroom." Let the child do the rest without help.
2. If the child was wet, circle the X on the form. If the child was not wet, do not circle the X.
3. If the child was wet, make the child change to clean bedclothes. The child must do as much of this without help as the child can do at bedtime. Then change the bedding. The child should do as much of this without help as he or she could do during the day. Then thank the child and put the child to bed again.
4. If the child was dry, thank the child and put the child to bed again after the trip to the bathroom.
5. Set the alarm for the next time you have to get the child up. When it rings, repeat the entire procedure.

6. The last time you wake the child before morning, check your record and see if the child was dry all night (no Xs circled). If the child was, post the Perfect Star (at the end of the chapter) in the child's room. Put a candy, sweet roll, or some favorite juice or dry cereal beside the child's bed where the child can find it in the morning. With and older child you can omit the reward if you feel it is inappropriate.

When to use Schedule 1. Start with Schedule 1, Day 1. Use this schedule for the five days indicated. If the child has been wet more than three different times on any night of these five, continue the program until you get five nights in a row with no more than three episodes of wetting the bed. Otherwise, after five nights go immediately to Schedule 2.

When to use the other schedules. You stay on Schedule 2 until for five nights in a row your child does not wet the bed at all. After Schedule 2 you go to Schedule 3. Use the same standard to move from Schedule 3 to 4, 4 to 5, and 5 to 6. Stay on Schedule 6 until you have three (or better yet, four) weeks of a completely dry bed.

Relapses. If, after you have been on a new schedule for at least three days, it becomes obvious that bedwetting has increased, you should move back one schedule. Then follow the procedures for that schedule as if you were starting it for the first time.

Finishing. After you complete Schedule 6, you should continue to check the child's bed in the morning. If the child is dry, give a reward. Continue this for at least three weeks after you no longer wake the child, and longer if you want.

Alarm Program

The alarm program works by teaching a child to wake up the minute he starts to urinate. After this has been in operation for some time, the child learns to anticipate urination and to wake up before urination starts.

The procedure works by using a very simple piece of apparatus. Two metal sheets of foil with numerous holes in them are separated by an insulated pad, and these are placed on the child's bed. A regular sheet may be placed over them. These sheets of foil are connected to an alarm apparatus. When the child makes even a few drops of urine it goes through the holes in the top sheet of foil and wets the insulating pad. This completes an extremely low-voltage electric circuit between the foil sheets and sounds the alarm. The noise of the alarm usually stops urination and wakes the child up. Only a small amount of urine is necessary to activate the alarm, so the alarm rings quickly once urination starts. No electric shock is given to the child; the amount of current used is not only safe, it is so small it cannot be felt, sensed, or have an effect on humans. No electricity goes through the child. Most commercial units use a minute amount of battery current to sense the urine and to sound the alarm.

Equipment. A commercial alarm unit must be purchased to carry out this program. Such a unit can be obtained relatively inexpensively from Sears, Roebuck and Company under the trademarked name "Wee-Alert." Sears also sells a more expensive model called the "Light Alert Buzzer." This unit uses a buzzer and a light to wake the sleeper. For a child who wakes with difficulty the added cost may be worth it. Both units are available on catalog order. Most parents have found Sears the most convenient source to obtain the alarm unit, although others may be available which are satisfactory.

Step 1. Familiarize yourself with the operation of the unit. Read the instructions carefully. Connect the unit according to the instructions and place it in the child's bed. Set the unit. Using a bit of salt water in a spoon, wet the sheet over the pads and make sure the alarm operates. Change the sheet, dry the pads, and reset the unit.

Step 2. Call your child into the room. Explain that this unit will help the child to remain dry at night by sounding an alarm when he or she starts to wet the bed. Say that like an alarm clock, this will wake the child up before the bed is really wet.

Step 3. This is a practice exercise for your child in using the alarm. Have your child set up the alarm, pad, and connections. Have the child set the alarm, spill some salt water from a spoon on the sheet to make the alarm ring, and turn off the alarm. Make the child walk into the bathroom, and then return. Explain that when the alarm rings at night, the child must turn off the alarm, go into the bathroom and finish urinating, and then return. Then have the child change the sheet (if necessary) and reset the alarm. Have the child practice this until the child can do it perfectly. Also have the child feel the pad while it is dry and while it is wet and the alarm is ringing.

Step 4. At the end of this chapter is the Star Club form. This should be posted by the child's bed. Each morning fill in the date and the day of the week. If the child has not wet the bed at all that night, glue a star in the space after "Day" or draw a star there. If the child has wet, just leave this space blank.

Step 5. At bedtime, have the child set the alarm before going to bed. When the alarm rings at night, the child must get up and go through the procedure which was practiced. One of the parents should also get up when the alarm rings to make sure that the child goes through the entire procedure. Make sure that the child is fully awake.

Step 6. Continue the procedures in Step 5 every night until the child is dry every morning for two consecutive weeks. This usually takes from four to eight weeks. The Star Club record will help you keep track.

Step 7. After two consecutive weeks without bedwetting you may have an occasional relapse. Each time there is a relapse of even one night you start the alarm program again, as in Step 5, and continue until there are two consecutive weeks without bedwetting as in Step 6.

This program has a very high rate of success if carried out correctly. If you have read the entire chapter you know that before starting the program you gave the "preparation and practice." You also know that you are giving your child liquids in the evening. You may also have started with a bladder training program. If you have done these things, success with the alarm program probably depends upon the following things. One is to make sure that the exact procedure is followed. Most important is that the child wake up fully, turn off the alarm without help, go to the bathroom after waking, change the sheets, and reset the alarm. Another factor which is probably important is using the procedure every night. A final important factor for long-range results is reinstating the procedure after relapses.

Final Comments

Many parents worry that curing bedwetting is likely to lead to the development of some other problem. Research on this has indicated that the effect is just the opposite. One researcher, using these procedures, obtained total cure in 74% of those treated, and marked improvement in another 15%. Personality tests and reports of teachers and parents showed no negative effects in any of those treated. In fact, children showed improvement in a number of areas other than bedwetting. The observation reported most often was the child's increased happiness on becoming dry. Many children were able to sleep overnight at friends or at camp for the first time. Other extensive reviews of similar procedures have supported the finding that side effects are positive.

BLADDER TRAINING RECORD

Date	Waiting Time	No Notification	Waited	Didn't Wait	Wet Bed	Dry Bed

ASSESSMENT
Regular Waking Program

Day	Bedtime	Hours After Bedtime											
		1	2	3	4	5	6	7	8	9	10	11	12
1													
2													
3													
4													
5													

INSTRUCTIONS

1. Each night, write down the child's bedtime.
2. Check the child's bed to see if it is wet or dry every hour after bedtime. Stop checking after a wet bed, or when the child gets up.
3. After five days, find the least "Hours After Bedtime" in which you found a wet bed. This is the "Start Time." It is _____ hours after bedtime.

BEGINNING PROGRAM
Regular Waking Program

The Start Time is ____ hours after bedtime.
The Waking Interval is ____ hours.

Day	Bedtime	1st Time	2nd Time	3rd Time	4th Time	5th Time	6th Time
				Get the child up			
1							
2							
3							
4							
5							
6							
7							
8							

9						
10						
11						
12						
13						
14						
15						

INSTRUCTIONS

1. Fill in the Start Time and the Waking Interval at the top.
2. Each night, fill in the time at which you put the child to bed.
3. Each night, add the Start Time to the bedtime. Write this time in the "1st Time" column. This is the first time you will wake the child that night.
4. After you have written down the first time, add the waking interval to the first time, and write it in the "2nd Time" column. Add the waking interval to the second time, and write it in the "3rd Time" column. Do this for all the rest of the times. These are the other times you will wake the child during the night.

SECOND PROGRAM
Regular Waking Program

The Old Start Time was _____ hours after bedtime.

The Waking Interval is _____ hours.

The New Start Time (Old Start Time plus one Waking Interval) is _____ hours after bedtime.

INSTRUCTIONS:

See beginning Program Form. The only difference is computing the Start Time for the first time to get the child up.

Day	Bedtime	Get the child up				
		1st Time	2nd Time	3rd Time	4th Time	5th Time
1						
2						
3						
4						

5	6	7	8	9	10	11	12	13	14	15

THE GOOD KID BOOK
THIRD PROGRAM
Regular Waking Program

The Old Start Time was____hours after bedtime.
The Waking Interval is____hours.
The New Start Time (Old Start Time plus one Waking Interval) is
____hours after bedtime.

INSTRUCTIONS

See Beginning Program Form. The only difference is computing the Start Time for the first time to get the child up.

Day	Bedtime	Get the child up			
		1st Time	2nd Time	3rd Time	4th Time
1					
2					
3					
4					
5					
6					
7					
8					
9					
10					
11					
12					
13					
14					
15					

FOURTH PROGRAM
Regular Waking Program

The Old Start Time was____hours after bedtime.
The Waking Interval is____hours.
The New Start Time (Old Start Time plus one Waking Interval) is
____hours after bedtime.

INSTRUCTIONS

See Beginning Program Form. The only difference is computing the Start Time for the first time to get the child up.

Day	Bedtime	Get the child up		
		1st Time	2nd Time	3rd Time
1				
2				
3				
4				
5				
6				
7				
8				
9				
10				
11				
12				
13				
14				
15				

THE GOOD KID BOOK
FIFTH PROGRAM
Regular Waking Program

The Old Start Time was_____hours after bedtime.
The Waking Interval is_____hours.
The New Start Time (Old Start Time plus one Waking Interval) is
_____hours after bedtime.

INSTRUCTIONS

See Beginning Program Form. The only difference is computing the Start Time for the first time to get the child up.

Day	Bedtime	Get the child up	
		1st Time	2nd Time
1			
2			
3			
4			
5			
6			
7			
8			
9			
10			
11			
12			
13			
14			
15			

SIXTH PROGRAM
Regular Waking Program

The Old Start Time was_____hours after bedtime.
The Waking Interval is_____hours.
The New Start Time (Old Start Time plus one Waking Interval) is
_____hours after bedtime.

INSTRUCTIONS

See Beginning Program Form. The only difference is computing the Start Time for the first time to get the child up.

		Get the child up
Day	Bedtime	1st Time
1		
2		
3		
4		
5		
6		
7		
8		
9		
10		
11		
12		
13		
14		
15		

THE GOOD KID BOOK
PERFECT

STAR CLUB

Date	Day		Date	Day		Date	Day	

VARIABLE WAKING SCHEDULE 1

Day	Bedtime	1	2	3	4	5	6	7	8	9	10	11
1		X	X		X			X	X		X	
2			X	X	X	X		X		X		X
3			X	X		X	X		X	X		
4		X		X	X		X		X		X	
5		X		X		X		X		X		X

VARIABLE WAKING SCHEDULE 2

Day	Bedtime	1	2	3	4	5	6	7	8	9	10	11
1		X	X		X			X			X	
2		X		X		X			X		X	
3			X			X	X			X		X
4			X				X	X				X
5		X		X		X			X	X		
6				X	X		X		X			X
7		X			X			X		X	X	
8			X	X		X	X				X	
9			X	X		X			X	X		
10		X			X			X				X

VARIABLE WAKING SCHEDULE 3

Day	Bedtime	1	2	3	4	5	6	7	8	9	10	11
1			X		X		X			X		
2		X			X			X			X	
3				X		X			X			X
4		X	X			X	X	X		X		
5				X	X				X			
6			X	X		X		X		X	X	
7		X										X
8					X	X			X		X	
9			X	X	X		X		X			X
10										X		

VARIABLE WAKING SCHEDULE 4

Day	Bedtime	1	2	3	4	5	6	7	8	9	10	11
1				X				X				X
2		X				X				X		
3				X			X			X		
4			X				X			X		
5				X			X				X	
6					X			X			X	
7			X		X			X				
8						X			X			X
9			X			X			X			
10		X			X				X			

VARIABLE WAKING SCHEDULE 5

Day	Bedtime	1	2	3	4	5	6	7	8	9	10	11
1				X					X			
2					X			X				
3												
4						X				X		
5					X		X					
6				X	X				X			
7				X			X					
8						X			X			
9							X			X		
10												

VARIABLE WAKING SCHEDULE 6

Day	Bedtime	1	2	3	4	5	6	7	8	9	10	11
1					X							
2						X						
3							X					
4				X								
5								X				
6						X	X					
7					X							
8												
9									X			
10								X				

12.
My Turn! My Turn!

IN cute storybooks about ideal families, problems are rare. In the evening the family sits around, the parents talk quietly, read, and pat the dog while the children play pleasantly on the living-room floor. One child says, "Wouldn't you like to try this puzzle for a little while, Jane? I've had it now for twenty minutes." "Oh, thank you, Mike, I would like to try it," says Jane, and with a smile Mike then hands it to Jane.

Are things really this nice? Well, sometimes, but not very often. More likely Jane says, "It's my turn to work the puzzle—you've had it for hours, you stingy brat," at which point Mike takes the whole puzzle, puts it in the box, and runs with it into his room, slamming the door after him. If he feels generous he may throw the puzzle at Jane.

Sharing things is a universal problem. Countries go to war over it. States fight in Congress over it. Adults go to court over it. We all know what children do. There are numerous explanations for why sharing is a problem. Some scientists claim the problem is linked to our evolution as a species, that we are born with an instinct to protect our "territory" from others. Other scientists relate sharing problems to toilet training or symbolic competition over parental affection. For our purposes, more practical observations are useful. What you don't share, you still have. The toy not given to another can still be played with. In addition, refusal to share is also a way to deliberately annoy another. Why these things are rewarding hardly matters. What matters is solving the problem of teaching young children to share, and that is what this chapter is about.

Whom Is This Program For?

Very few children actively play with other children before age one and a half, and in many real play does not develop until sometime between ages two and three. So in very young children, selfishness is normal. However, a continuation of this behavior at age three or older suggests that parental intervention will be useful. Of course, we should realize that at all ages children are frequently selfish—in fact, adults are not always good at sharing things either. But even if the behavior is not unusual, it is still not pleasant, and parental effort to improve such behavior is worthwhile. A child who is very reluctant to share anything, and who creates unpleasantness in such situations, may find it more difficult to make or keep friends.

This program is designed for children between the ages of three and thirteen. It may work with children who are slightly younger or older; you can certainly give it a try without any undesirable effects.

How to Start

In this chapter you are shown how to teach children six different skills. These are:

1. Offering to share.
2. Responding correctly to an offer to share.
3. Appropriate ways to ask to share something.
4. Responding correctly to a request to share.
5. Actually sharing.
6. Correct responses when allowed to share.

In addition, a simple procedure is described for you to follow when inappropriate sharing behavior occurs.

You will explicitly teach each of the six skills, step by step. For each skill you will also learn how to help your children maintain the skill. So for every skill you will go through two steps: (1) explicit teaching, and (2) maintenance in practice.

Before starting any part of this program, read the entire chapter. Then come back to the section on "offering to share," and start the program.

Offering to Share

The first skill taught is "offering to share." This means saying things like "Want to try this?" or "Your turn now," or any similar remarks which invite sharing.

Explicit teaching. This is taught only to the child for whom sharing is a problem. Some of the later skills you will teach to all the children with whom your child is playing. The teaching procedure you will use is called "prompt-model-reinforce." "Prompt" means you tell the child what is to be done, "model" means that you demonstrate how to act, and "reinforce" means that you reward the child for doing it.

Step 1. In this step you teach the child how to share with you.

1. Sit down alone with your child shortly before he will be playing with other children.
2. Hold two or three toys which you suspect your child might sometimes be reluctant to share with others.
3. Tell your child, "I am going to show you how to share toys so your friends will like playing with you better."
4. Start playing with one of the toys and after a few seconds say, "Would you like a turn?"
5. Immediately give your child the toy.
6. Prompt and model. After a minute or two say, "Now you share. Say to me, 'Would you like a turn?' "
7. If your child does not offer you a turn (however it is worded), repeat the prompting firmly, using the child's name. Do this until the child responds.
8. Reinforce. When your child responds with a sharing offer, reward the child at once. Say, "Thank you for sharing." Do this immediately, whether or not your child actually gives you the toy. At this stage ignore whether or not the toy is given. If it is, accept it. If not, ignore it. But make sure you immediately reinforce your child for offering. If you wish, carry some small candies and give the child one of them as you thank the child.
9. Repeat the entire procedure (numbers 4-8) with each of the toys several times. Then take your child to play with his friends.

Go through this explicit teaching at least three times on three separate occasions, each time shortly before your child is going to play with friends. If your child has any reluctance making offers to share with you, continue the explicit teaching until it disappears. Then go on to Step 2.

Step 2. In this step you teach your child to make offers to share with friends.

1. When your child is playing with friends, you should remain present.
2. Prompt and model. Carefully watch your child playing. When you see that your child has played with some toy for a few minutes and no longer seems very interested in it, say, "Ask if [other child's name] would like a turn. Say, '[other child's name], do you want to play with this now?' "
3. If your child does not make an offer to share with the other child, repeat the prompting firmly, using your child's name to make sure you have his or her attention. Do this until your child responds correctly.
4. When your child responds with a sharing offer, reinforce with praise (and a candy if you desire) at once. Say, "Thank you for offering to share." Again, ignore whether or not your child actually offers the toy.
5. Repeat numbers 2-4 five or six times while the children are playing.

Go through this explicit teaching on at least three separate occasions when your child is playing with others. If the child has any problems in making offers to share, continue the explicit teaching until the problems are eliminated.

Maintenance in practice. You should use this procedure with *all* children in your child's play group. A "group" in this chapter merely means two or more children. Do not prompt or model. Whenever you hear your child or another child make an offer to share, you should reinforce it. You should do this with praise statements such as "I like the way you offer to share," or, if you desire, with candies. Sometimes make the praise specific and name the child who made the offer (e.g., "Frank, you are very generous"), and sometimes make it general (e.g., "My, you all are very generous children"). Use the following schedule.

1. For the first three play periods after you complete explicit teaching, spend at least ten minutes watching your child play with friends. Reinforce every offer to share that you hear. Again, ignore whether or not the toy is actually offered.

2. After these three periods, try occasionally to reinforce offers to share. If you cannot spend time continually watching the children, walk through and listen for a minute or two. If you are in some other location but can hear the children playing, occasionally stop what you are doing and listen for offers to share. Whichever you do, try to reinforce the instant you hear an offer. Try to do this from time to time during your child's play.

Responses to Offers to Share

When a child offers to share something with another child, one factor which may affect whether or not the child will do this again is how the second child responds. In this section you teach all the children in your child's group how to respond to offers to share.

Explicit teaching. This teaching is done while your child is playing with friends, and after you have completed teaching the first set of skills. It is done with all the children present. It does not matter if different children are present on different occasions.

1. For at least fifteen minutes, stay, watch, and listen while your child plays with friends. Continue to reinforce offers to share.
2. If a child offers to share something, listen to what the child to whom the offer is made says.
3. Prompt and model. If the child to whom the offer is made does not thank the offerer in some way, say, "Frank, thank Susan for being generous. Say, 'Thank you for the puzzle.'"
4. If the child does not thank the offerer appropriately, repeat the request more firmly, stressing the child's name. Do this until the child responds correctly.
5. Reinforce. When the child does thank the first child, say something like "That's the way we do it!"
6. Continue to prompt, model, and reinforce children for correct responses to offers until you have reinforced eight or ten such responses or until fifteen minutes are up.

Do this explicit teaching on three separate occasions. Continue it longer if children are not regularly thanking those who offer to share with them until this is no longer a problem. While you are doing this occasionally reinforce offers to share also.

Maintenance in practice. This is exactly the same as the maintenance in practice for offers to share. Do not prompt or model. Whenever you hear a correct response to an offer to share, reinforce it, using statements such as you did during the explicit teaching. If you want, use candies. Continue to praise offers to share from time to time. Use the following schedule:

1. Do this for the first three play periods after explicit teaching, for at least ten consecutive minutes each time. Reinforce every appropriate response to offers to share, and occasional offers to share. Again, ignore whether or not a toy or object is actually shared.
2. Then switch to occasional reinforcement for both offers to share and for correct responses to offers to share by walking through the play area every few minutes, or by listening from a distance. Reinforce immediately after the behavior.

Sharing

Sharing means actually giving another child a toy or object. It does not matter if the other child requested this or whether an offer was made.

Explicit teaching. This is taught only to your child.

Step 1. In this step you teach the child how to act with just you present.

1. Sit down alone with your child shortly before he will be playing with others.
2. Hold two or three toys which you suspect your child might sometimes be reluctant to share with other children.
3. Tell your child, "I am going to show you some more about sharing toys."
4. Model. Start playing with one of the toys. After a few seconds you hand the toy to your child and say, "Your turn."
5. Prompt. After a minute or two reach out your hand and say, "My turn, hand it to me."
6. If the child does not give you the toy, repeat number 5 again firmly, using your child's name. Do this until the child responds.
7. Reinforce. When your child hands you the toy say, "Thank you for sharing." Do this the instant the child starts to hand you the toy, while you are still taking it. If you want, use candies.
8. Then play with one of the toys for a second and this time say, "Would you like to play with this?"

9. If the child says yes, hand the child the toy. If the child says no, play with one of the other toys and repeat until the child says yes.
10. Reinforce. Reinforce your child if he or she thanks you for the offer.
11. Prompt and model. Then say, "Now you share. Ask me if I would like a turn."
12. If your child does not offer you a toy, repeat firmly until the child does.
13. When your child offers you a toy, say, "yes," and reach for the toy. Take the toy if it is not actually offered.
14. As you get the toy, say something like "Thanks, I appreciate your generosity."
15. Repeat this entire procedure (numbers 4-14) with each of the toys several times. You will note that sometimes sharing is preceded by an offer to share, and sometimes it is not. If you prompt your child to make an offer to share but he shares directly without first making an offer, treat this as correct and reinforce the child.

Go through this explicit teaching at least three times on three separate occasions which occur shortly before your child is to play with friends. If there are any problems over sharing with you, continue the procedure until your child shares without a problem. Then go on to Step 2.

Step 2. In this step you teach your child to share with friends.

1. When your child is playing with friends you should remain present.
2. Watch your child carefully and when your child has played with something for a few minutes and no longer seems interested in it say, "Share your toy with [name a child close to your child]."
3. If your child does not comply, repeat the request firmly, using your child's name. Do this until your child complies.
4. When your child does share, reinforce the child immediately with praise and/or candy.
5. Occasionally, instead of prompting your child to share, prompt him to offer to share. Say something like "Ask [adjacent child] if he would like to play with [name of toy]."
6. If the other child says no, reinforce your child for offering. If

the other child says yes, reinforce your child only if your child actually shares.

7. Repeat numbers 1-6 five or six times. Most of the time prompt your child to share something directly; sometimes, however, prompt your child to offer to share something.

Go through this explicit teaching on three separate occasions. If your child has trouble sharing with friends, continue this explicit teaching longer until it is no longer a problem.

Maintenance in practice. This is exactly the same as the maintenance in practice for the first two skills, and is done when your child is with friends. Do not prompt or model. Regularly reinforce sharing by your child and any other child. Occasionally reinforce offers to share, but only if the child actually follows through and shares. Occasionally reinforce correct responses to offers to share. Use the following schedule:

1. Do this for the first three play periods after explicit teaching for at least ten consecutive minutes each time.
2. Then continue to reinforce occasionally as you have done in the other Maintenance in Practice sessions.

Responses to Sharing

When a child shares something with another, the other child's responses may influence future behavior. In this section you teach all the children your child is playing with to respond correctly to sharing.

Explicit teaching. This teaching is done when your child is playing with other children and is done with whatever children are present.

1. For at least fifteen minutes watch and listen while your child plays with friends. Continue to occasionally reinforce sharing, offers to share which are followed by actual sharing, and correct responses to offers.
2. If one child shares something with another, listen to what the other says.
3. If the second child thanks the first, say something like "My, you're nice and polite."
4. If the second child does not thank the first say, "Frank, thank Susan for being so generous."
5. If the child does not respond properly, repeat the request firmly until the child does.

6. When the child does thank the first child say something like "Very good, [child's name]."
7. Continue numbers 2-6 for at least fifteen minutes.

Do this explicit teaching on three separate play occasions. Continue it longer if you have any problems getting children (especially your child) to thank others for sharing. While you are doing this, occasionally reinforce sharing and responses to offers to share.

Maintenance in practice. This is exactly the same as the previous maintenance in practice techniques. Do not prompt or model. Reinforce correct responses to sharing, correct responses to offers to share, and sharing behavior itself. Do not reinforce offers to share unless the child follows through and shares or unless the other child says no to the offer. Use the following schedule:

1. Do this continuously for at least fifteen minutes for three play sessions after explicit teaching. Reinforce all correct responses to sharing and occasionally reinforce the other types of behavior.
2. As you have done after teaching other skills then switch to occasional reinforcement for all these types of behavior.

Appropriate Requests to Share Something and Responding to Appropriate Requests

Some children do not know how to ask another for something appropriately. They may just grab. They may just point. They may cry. They may yell something like "Give me that" or "My turn," or whatever. Such approaches do not increase the probability of desirable sharing behavior.

Explicit teaching. This is taught to all children who happen to be present in a play group. There must be at least one child with your child.

1. Watch and listen carefully to the children playing.
2. If a child asks nicely for something from another, reinforce the child. Say something like "My, you asked nicely."
3. Reinforce the other child if he or she gives the first child the object.
4. If a child grabs, yells, or tries to get something in some other

inappropriate way, say very firmly, "[Child's name], stop! Ask nicely, Say, 'May I please have a turn with that?' "

5. If the child does not do this, repeat it more firmly, using the child's name until the child does. If this does not work, remove the child from the group for two minutes.

6. If the child finally does ask nicely, reinforce the child for asking appropriately. Say something like "I like the way you asked for that."

7. If a child asks for something appropriately and as a result another child does share something, reinforce the child who shared also.

8. Repeat numbers 1-7 until you have reinforced appropriate requests for at least fifteen minutes.

Repeat this procedure on three different occasions. If most children are not requesting things appropriately, continue the procedure longer until this is no longer a problem. Make sure your child is performing well before stopping.

Maintenance in practice. This is exactly the same as previous maintenance in practice technique. The behavior which you are trying to strengthen includes: (1) sharing, (2) correct responses to sharing, (3) correct responses to offers to share, (4) appropriate requests, and finally (5) correct responses to appropriate requests.

1. For three play sessions reinforce all appropriate requests to share and positive responses to requests to share, as well as occasionally reinforcing other types of sharing behavior.

2. After three such sessions, switch to occasional reinforcement of all sharing behavior taught as you have done after explicit teaching of other skills.

Fights and Serious Arguments over Sharing

At any time before, during, or after you have completed this program there may be fights or loud arguments over sharing. Whenever this occurs you should respond in the same way: remove the article which is the source of the trouble.

1. With children between three and six say, "You can't have this if it is going to cause trouble." Then remove the article. After ten minutes return it without comment.

2. With children age six through about nine, remove the article without making any comment and return it without comment in thirty minutes.
3. With older children remove the article without comment and return it in the same way in an hour.

No other procedures are necessary. For this to succeed, only two things are usually necessary: (1) to do it every time there is trouble, and (2) to do it the moment trouble starts.

Final Comments

In this program you improved sharing behavior by teaching separately several of the components which contribute to what we call sharing. Using the prompt-model-reinforce technique of explicit teaching you taught your child and others your child plays with:

• To offer to share playthings.
• To respond in a positive way to sharing offers from other children.
• To ask for a turn appropriately.
• To respond in a positive way for requests for a turn with a plaything.
• To actually let others share playthings.
• To respond positively when another lets them share.

For each of these you first taught the actual skill and then you gave reinforced practice in the skill in a play situation. Since your interest was mainly in improving your own child's skills, sometimes you taught your child only. Where it was necessary, you taught your child as well as your child's friends. In addition, you learned a simple technique for handling squabbles over sharing.

To keep this good behavior going you should occasionally reinforce all the components as you did in the final maintenance in practice sessions.

Notice that your teaching technique never involved nagging or criticizing; it emphasized teaching the right way to do things and reinforcing good behavior. Negative approaches such as nagging may sometimes work in the short run, but they hardly ever work in the long run, and frequently create as much unpleasantness as they are designed to cure.

You probably also noticed that you taught one small thing at a time, rather than trying to do the whole thing at once. This step-by-step approach is one important factor in guaranteeing success. By proceeding in this manner you can increase the probability that the children will be able to do what you are teaching them, and that failure will not result in nagging and unpleasantness.

13.
Good Grooming

CHILDREN and adults frequently disagree about what constitutes good grooming. Sometimes children consider good grooming trivial, a waste of time. And some adults persistently confuse the needs of cleanliness and health with style or fashion. As parents, we should try to remember that long hair or odd colors of clothing are not serious matters of health—either moral or physical. Generally speaking, parents who attempt to force their children to conform to dress and hair styles which conflict with what is current among the children's peers will create more problems than they solve. So, this chapter will not cover problems of style of dress or hair length. It will cover basic cleanliness and grooming, those things which may affect health or which may offend other people who must come into contact with the individual.

Some of the topics covered here are obviously only applicable to older children; others will apply mostly to younger children. The entire chapter is arranged so that parents can select the specific programs they need. If you do not agree that all goals presented in this chapter are desirable, omit those with which you disagree. If you do not know whether or not certain issues are actually related to health, consult your physician or some other source of information on health practices and personal hygiene.

Parents frequently assume that the right way to bathe, wash, etc. is so obvious that explicit instruction is not necessary. On other topics, parents feel awkward or embarrassed about directly teaching their children necessary skills, for example how to wipe after a bowel movement, how to wash certain parts of the body, or to perform the hygienic procedures related to menstruation. These things must be taught, and that is what this chapter will help you do.

From the list of grooming tasks presented here each parent will select the topics which need work. In some families this may only be one of two topics; in others it may be several. For each task, a specific teaching procedure, done only once in a single brief session, is described. Once the teaching is done, the list of grooming tasks is posted in a private place. Each family will decide upon some daily consequence for satisfactory completion of all items on the list. If every item is completed, the reward is given. However, if a child does not complete the task without help in a satisfactory manner, the child can still get credit by going through a short positive practice exercise for that task. If this is done, credit is also given. If neither is done, there is no reward. The positive practice procedure helps teach correct behavior and weaken incorrect behavior. In addition, it provides a second chance for a child who forgets.

Whom Is This Program For?

If your child is old enough to take responsibility for bathing, showering, hand washing, tooth brushing, etc., and any of these are a problem, you can use this program. The age at which you will be able to use this program depends upon the child. If the child is cooperative and not resentful and the problems are mainly those of "forgetfulness" there is probably no age limit. If the child is uncooperative, success will probably depend upon whether or not you have some reasonable rewards you can provide which you feel are appropriate and which will reinforce the correct behavior. This will be discussed in a later section. Read the entire program, and then begin.

Grooming Skills Covered

Go through the list of grooming skills described in the following material, and decide which of them are serious enough problems for you to include in your program. If you decide that you wish to include a topic in your program, write it on the Good Grooming List at the end of the chapter and fill in the additional information required on that form.

Bathing or showering. Many parents become upset because their children do not bathe or shower often enough. If you wish to include this task you must decide the following:

1. Do you care whether or not your child takes a bath rather than a shower? With children who are old enough, I suggest you leave this up to the child if facilities are available. If you do not care, on the form list "Bath or shower." If you do care, write one or the other. If you wish your child to take a bath on certain days and a shower on others, list each separately as two different tasks.
2. How often do you feel bathing or showering is necessary—that is, what is your minimum requirement? If you want this done daily, check it for every day of the week by making an X in the correct boxes. If less often, decide on which days you want it done rather than listing "Three times a week." If you wish to list options for when a task may be done this is satisfactory, as long as your listing is unambiguous.
3. How will you decide if a bath or a shower has been taken? This will depend upon your child. If you are satisfied with the child's word, mark "Child's word" in the "How Check" column. If you will be satisfied merely by checking the tub or shower, mark this. If you wish to hear the bath and shower in progress, mark this. Mark any method which will satisfy you that a bath or shower has been taken.
4. The last decision is the time of day. Mark a specific time in that column, or, if you don't care about the time, just write "Any time."

Shampooing hair. The procedure here is the same as for bathing or showering. You must decide how often and when this must be done, and how you will check. Mark these on the form.

Combing and/or brushing hair. If your child's hair is clean, concern over neatness will be much less important and perhaps you will feel satisfied without requiring combing and/or brushing. If not, you will probably want to specify that this should be done daily and, in the "When" column, that it should be done before leaving for school. The only reasonable ways to check are to look at the results or to observe the actual combing and brushing. Make it clear that your opinion will be final, and then be very lenient; if the hair shows any indication that it has been attended to, mark it as OK.

Clean nails and hands. With this problem, it is probably easier to check the results rather than the process. If so, in the "How Check" column write "Look at hands." You will probably want this done daily, so check everyday. You may wish it done more than once a day. For instance, you may want to check this before breakfast and before dinner. If so, mark "Breakfast and dinner" under "When."

Clean face. Treat this in the same manner as you did nails and hands.

Deodorant. Depending upon your child's age, activities, and other factors you may want him or her to use an underarm deodorant. If so, you will probably want this done every day. Even if it is not necessary every day, your child will find it easier to remember to do it if it is a daily task. Again, you must decide upon some method of checking. You may take your child's word, directly observe your child applying the deodorant, or, if the deodorant has a scent, check by smell. It is obvious that you will want your child to use the deodorant before dressing.

Makeup (too much). A touchy subject, but it can be dealt with. It is probably easier to handle this problem by requiring that makeup purchased be approved by you before it is paid for than by arguing over what is appropriate for any day. If you do decide to include this as a grooming task, you may have to list it several times as several different tasks—once for morning before going to school and separately for after school or going out in the evening. List these and the days, perhaps having "A.M. Makeup" and "P.M. Makeup" as two separate topics. Checking is very difficult, and likely to cause arguments, but try the following. With your daughter go to a store which sells magazines or look at magazines you have available. Select a color photograph of a model or movie star, or an illustration from an article on use of makeup which is acceptable to you and your child as indicating the maximum amount of makeup acceptable. Buy the magazine and keep the photograph. When you check, compare your daughter's makeup with the picture. You will have to arbitrarily say that if in your opinion she has more makeup on than the individual in the photo, it is not acceptable. This is probably about the best you can do.

Clean clothes. With styles what they are among children, it is probably best to stress cleanliness only and ignore wrinkles. It is probably also best to ignore (as a daily issue) polished shoes. You will probably require clean clothes every day, so check each day on the Good Grooming List. There are two ways you can check. The first is by inspection—appearance and smell. The second is by how long the clothes have been worn, e.g., you may decide that socks and underwear must be clean every day, shirts must be clean every other day, jeans less often, and so forth. If you do this, you will have to keep notes on what is worn and check each day.

Tooth brushing. If this is one of the grooming tasks you want to include, determine how often and when it is to be done. Mark on the form with Xs the days when this is required, and mark the times it is required under "When." For most people it is easiest to check a child's tooth brushing before breakfast and before bedtime, so you may wish to indicate this under "When." Finally, fill in the "How Check" column. You may decide to actually observe your child do the brushing. You may just check to see if the toothbrush is wet (although many parents have been fooled by this). You may feel that you can determine this by checking your child's mouth.

Menstruation. Some parents of adolescent girls are concerned over proper hygiene during menstruation. Topics of concern may be ordinary washing, the use of sanitary napkins or tampons, or washing and changing clothes if this is made necessary by the sudden unexpected onset of a menstrual period. These difficulties require some learning of new skills. A natural, matter-of-fact approach will prevent or solve many problems. If your girl needs help with learning or remembering proper grooming at these times you may include some of these topics in the grooming list. List the specific tasks which are problems on the Good Grooming List rather than the general topic of "menstruation." For instance, if the major problem is that your girl does not change clothes if this becomes necessary with the sudden onset of a period, list this specifically: "Changing clothes if necessary when a period comes on suddenly." Since it is only necessary when the problem occurs, under "When" merely mark "When necessary and possible." Checking will usually involve inspecting clothes.

Cleanliness after bowel movements. Many younger children do not wipe adequately after a bowel movement. Sometimes this is a result of impatience, but frequently they just haven't been taught what is necessary. Usually parents become aware of this problem when they see the child's underwear, although it may also be detected at bath time or sometimes by smell.

Most, but not all children have a bowel movement every day. With those who are less regular it is difficult to predict those days on which a bowel movement will occur. Therefore, it is best to mark all seven days of the week for this task if it is one you need to include. Under "How Check" you will probably want to list "Check underwear," or

"In bath" (if you bathe the child), or possibly "Smell." Under "When" you will probably want to list "All the time," meaning that the child will lose credit or have to go through a positive practice procedure anytime you detect a problem of this sort.

If there are grooming problems which are of concern to you and which have not been mentioned, you may add them to the list and try to develop procedures for them yourself.

Go over the Good Grooming List once more and delete any items which you feel are really trivial; the shorter the list the better. For each item you should have indicated the days of the week during which your child must complete this grooming skill, the manner in which you will determine or check to see if it was done, and the times by which it should be done.

Deciding on Rewards and Explaining the Program

At this point, show your child the Good Grooming List and the Reward List at the end of the chapter. The first you have already filled out. Go over each item on the Good Grooming List and explain exactly what he or she will have to do, and when, and how you will check. Tell the child that a point will be earned for every day on which *all* of these tasks are done perfectly without your reminding or correcting. Make clear that if even *one* is not done correctly, no point will be earned. However, tell your child that if a task is missed the first time, a point can still be earned if your child will immediately practice the skill for several minutes in a way that you will describe when the time comes. Make sure that your child understands that even if one or more tasks are forgotten or done incorrectly, the point can still be earned by positive practice. Also make clear that the practice is voluntary. To get a point a practice will have to be done for each task missed or all tasks must be done correctly without practice or reminders.

Now show your child the Reward List. You and the child must now negotiate some reasonable rewards. In doing this remember that only 1 point can be earned per day for a maximum of 7 points per week. Your child's age will affect which rewards are appropriate. Undoubtedly you and your child can come up with many useful ideas not on this list, but these are some suggestions.

1. *Later bedtime.* For instance, you may decide that your child can stay up fifteen minutes later for each point earned. This may necessitate restricting the number of points which can be saved up and spent in one night.
2. *Extra allowance.* You may decide that you are willing to give so much extra allowance for each point earned during the week.
3. *Things related to grooming.* If your child desires some new clothes, makeup, after-shave, a new comb and brush, etc., you can have your child earn them through points. For instance, you might decide that a certain new shirt, belt, or piece of jewelry can be purchased for 20 points.
4. *Privileges.* Similarly, you may let your children earn special privileges by setting a point value for them.

Now assign point costs to each reward. Try to be generous enough to make going through the program worthwhile. Seven points should be able to purchase something which is not trivial. For larger rewards —a new blouse, for example—you may assign a value that will require saving up points for several weeks. When you and your child have decided on several rewards, list the rewards and their point values on the Reward List at the end of the chapter.

Now show your child the Grooming Summary at the end of the chapter. Explain that on each day you will list the date in the first column. The numbers 1, 2, 3, 4, and 5 refer to the tasks on the Good Grooming List. When a task is done perfectly or the practice is completed, you will check it. If a task is not done correctly and a positive practice is not completed, write a zero under the number for that task. At the end of the day you will then write "Yes" or "No" under "Credit." A "Yes" will mean that each task on the Good Grooming List was done perfectly or the positive practice was done for that task, indicated by all checks. A "No" will mean there was at least one zero. You will then write the total points your child now has, keeping track as you would in a checkbook.

Tell your child that to help him or her earn the points you are going to quickly teach the correct way to do each task before starting the program (the explicit teaching).

Now you have only one task before starting the explicit teaching. Post the Good Grooming List, the Reward List, and the Grooming Summary in some spot where you and your child can see it easily, but where it is private and not available to other people. Show it to your child, explaining that it will be there at all times in case he or she

wishes to check anything. Also make clear that you will explain anything about the program if there are questions now or at some later
time.

Starting Explicit Teaching

In the later sections on each skill explicit teaching procedures are
described. Even if your child actually knows how to do the task, you
should go through the explicit teaching for every task you have included on the Good Grooming List. If your child actually can do the
task the explicit teaching will take only a few minutes.

Start by doing the explicit teaching for that task which you feel
will be most difficult for your child to learn. If you do not expect any
to be difficult, start with the one which bothers you the most. You
will probably be able to do all of the tasks you selected in an hour or
two; however, you need not do all at once or even on the same day
if you feel that your child is losing interest. Try to do all the explicit
teaching in two consecutive days. The explicit teaching is done only
once, before starting the rest of the program.

Running the Program

To run the program, complete the following steps each day:

1. Check for correct completion of each task on the Good Grooming List when you are supposed to do so.
2. If it is done correctly mark a check for that task for that day on
   the Grooming Summary. The task numbers are the same as on
   the Good Grooming List.
3. If it is not correct, offer your child a chance to do the positive
   practice. If your child refuses, mark a zero for that task for the
   day on the Grooming Summary.
4. If your child decides to do the positive practice, look up the
   positive practice procedure for that task in the sections which
   follow and have your child do it. If your child completes the
   practice, make a check for that task the same as if your child
   had done it correctly the first time.
5. At the end of the day, if all the tasks on the Grooming Summary are checked, mark "Yes" under "Credit" and add it to
   yesterday's balance to give the total. If there were any zeros
   mark "No" and make the total the same as yesterday's balance.

6. Check to see if your child has spent any points today. If so, subtract them from the total and write in the new balance. If no, points were spent the total and the balance will be the same.

Now let's look at the explicit teaching and positive practice procedures for each of the types of grooming.

Bathing and/or Showering

Explicit teaching. In this procedure, you observe your child taking one bath or shower, instruct the child specifically on each thing that should be done, and then check to make sure each thing is done correctly. If the child is older and you feel there might be some embarrassment with direct observation, you can do this verbally through a shower curtain or the bathroom door. Instruct the child to do each of the things on the list which follows and by direct observation or verbal report make sure each is done. The instructions should work equally well with a bath or shower.

1. Have the child adjust the water so it is relatively warm. You should check this by hand.
2. Have the child get thoroughly wet. In the bath this should not be a problem.
3. Have your child soap all of the body thoroughly. Make sure places like armpits, genital areas, buttocks, and between buttocks are included. (You instruct and check or ask about *each* explicitly.) Make sure the face is washed.
4. Rinse thoroughly.

Positive practice. This procedure is carried out when the child does not bathe or shower at the indicated time and chooses the positive practice to earn the point.

1. The child should go to the bathroom and remove clothes as if for a bath or shower.
2. The child should then stand in the tub or shower without turning on the water.
4. The child should get dressed again.
5. The above procedure should be repeated five times. You must check that this is done.
6. On the sixth time, the child should actually take a shower or bath.

This may seem excessive, and many children will think the positive practice is just a game in the beginning. However, it will work if it is done.

Shampooing

Explicit teaching. Have your child go to the bath, shower, or sink for a shampoo. The child should be wearing whatever clothes he or she usually wears during a shampoo. Make sure the child brings the shampoo.

1. Have the child turn on and adjust the water for the shampoo.
2. Have the child thoroughly wet the hair.
3. Have the child lather up completely.
4. Have the child rinse completely.
5. Repeat procedures 3 and 4 if necessary.
6. Repeat procedures 3 and 4 using a hair rinse if necessary.
7. Have the child end by rinsing the hair very thoroughly.

You must check to make sure every step is done.
Positive practice. Go through the following steps.

1. The child should go to the bathroom and remove clothes as for a shampoo.
2. The child should get all shampoo (and rinse, if used) ready, as if for a shampoo.
3. The child should get in the tub or shower if these are used, or stand over the sink if this is used.
4. The child should then put everything away and get dressed again.
5. Repeat procedures 1-4 five times.
6. Repeat procedures 1-4 one more time. On this trial the child should actually shampoo.

You must check to make sure each step is completed.

Clean Nails and Hands

Explicit teaching. Have the child go to the sink and roll up sleeves or remove a shirt or blouse if necessary. Have the child get soap and a nail brush if necessary.

1. The child should fill the sink with warm water, hot enough for the job.

2. Under your supervision, have the child do a thorough job of nail and hand cleaning.
3. Have the child dry and clean up the area.

Positive practice. Supervise each of the following steps to make sure that they are done. As with showering, bathing, and shampooing actual washing is done only once.

1. The child should go to the sink and roll up or remove clothes as necessary.
2. The child should get soap and a brush, if desired, ready.
3. The child should put an inch of cool water in the sink and briefly "fake" washing and scrubbing nails.
4. The child should empty the sink, dry hands, replace clothes, and put materials away.
5. Repeat procedures 1-4 five times.
6. Repeat procedures 1-4 one more time. This time, the child should actually clean the hands and nails.

Combing and/or Brushing Hair

Explicit teaching. Have the child comb or brush the hair under your supervision. Make sure this is done correctly. If it is not, make the child repeat it until it is.

Positive practice. Have the child go to wherever the child should have combed and/or brushed his hair in the first place.

1. Have the child comb and/or brush the hair correctly.
2. Have the child mess up the hair.
3. Have the child go back to wherever it was that you checked the hair and found it unsatisfactory.
4. Have the child return to wherever the hair is usually combed and/or brushed.
5. Repeat procedures 1-4 five times.
6. Repeat procedures 1-4 one more time, except on this step have the child stop when the hair is combed or brushed.

Washing Face

Explicit teaching. Supervise the child during face washing. Make sure that the face is wet, that it is thoroughly soaped (including around ears, neck, etc.), and that it is then thoroughly rinsed. Finally, make sure the child dries well.

Positive practice. When you check the child's face and it is not clean, have the child go to the location where he should have washed.

1. Have the child run a small amount of water in the sink.
2. Have the child splash water on his or her face.
3. Have the child dry and run the water out of the sink.
4. Have the child return to the location where you decided that the face was dirty.
5. Repeat procedures 1-4 five times.
6. Repeat procedures 1-4 once more, but on this repeat have the child actually wash his or her face.

Deodorant

Explicit teaching. Deodorant should be applied only after the armpits have been washed in a bath or shower. Therefore you will have to do the explicit teaching after a bath or a shower. If the child would be embarrassed by your presence, have the child dress enough to avoid this (i.e. pants for a male, a skirt, and possibly bra for a female).

1. Have the child take out whatever form of deodorant is used.
2. Have the child apply the deodorant to the underarm area.
3. Check carefully to make sure that the entire underarm area is covered.
4. Also check carefully to make sure that an excessive amount of deodorant is not used. If too much liquid roll-on or spray deodorant is used, staining or damage to clothing may result.
5. If the deodorant is a type which does not dry instantly, make the child allow drying time before completing dressing.

Positive practice. If failure to use deodorant occurs along with failure to bathe or shower, combine the procedures. That is, have the child go through the positive practice procedures for bathing or showering once, then the deodorant positive practice and then the repeats of the two combined procedures.

1. From wherever you have checked and found that the child has failed to use deodorant, have the child return to the location where the deodorant should have been applied.
2. Have the child get out the deodorant.
3. Have the child remove shirt, blouse, or whatever is necessary to use the deodorant.

4. Have the child open the deodorant and hold it to the under-arm area without actually applying the deodorant.
5. Have the child close and put away the deodorant, dress, and return to the area where you checked for deodorant use.
6. Repeat procedures 1-5 five times.
7. Repeat once more, but this time have the child actually apply the deodorant.

Too Much Makeup

Explicit teaching. Have the young lady get out all makeup that will be used. Check to see if anything is included that is not appropriate. Explain why this is inappropriate. Have your girl apply makeup slowly step by step as you supervise. If she starts to apply too much, stop her instantly. Explain how it will look and how it will not match the photograph you both selected which sets the standard. Continue this until she applies makeup correctly.

Positive practice. When you check your girl's face, if the makeup is excessive relative to the standard photo you have adopted, point this out, describing exactly what there is too much of. Then have her return to wherever she applies makeup.

1. Using soap and water or cleansing cream, or both, have her remove all the makeup.
2. Have her get out all the makeup she should use for this occasion.
3. Step by step, have her verbally describe what makeup she should apply and how much.
4. Have her put the makeup away.
5. Have your girl return to wherever you checked and decided that there was too much makeup. Then have her return to where she applies makeup.
6. Repeat procedures 2-5 five times.
7. Repeat once more, but have your daughter actually apply the correct amount of makeup on this final repeat.

Clean Clothes

Explicit teaching. Obtain a pair of dirty jeans and a pair of clean jeans. Obtain a dirty and clean pair of each article of clothing which your child wears daily. Place all of them on the child's bed. Call your child in. Go over each pair, first the clean item of the pair, then the dirty item of the pair. Point out the exact differences in each—dirty spots, wrinkles, stains, and so forth. If you are checking on the Good Grooming List according to how many times an item has been worn, with each item explain how many times it should be worn before it is changed. For instance, after showing your child the difference between a dirty sock and a clean sock say, "Socks should be changed every morning. Wear a clean pair of socks every morning." Have your child repeat this back to you.

Positive practice. If your child shows up at the check time wtih dirty clothes, go through the following positive practice.

1. Name each item which is dirty and describe why it is dirty. Say "This has a stain on it," or, "You are supposed to change your shirt at least every other day."
2. Have your child return to his or her room and dress in clean clothes. Then have the child undress and put the dirty ones on again.
3. Have the child return to where you checked the clothes.
4. Repeat procedures 1-3 five times.
5. Repeat procedures 1-3 one additional time, but on this final time have your child leave the clean clothes on and return to the check spot wearing clean clothes.

Tooth Brushing

Explicit teaching. Get your toothbrush, your child's toothbrush, the toothpaste used, and floss if it is used.

1. Demonstrate how to wet the brush and apply paste with your brush.
2. Have the child do exactly the same thing using his or her brush.
3. Demonstrate the correct brushing motions, making sure you brush your teeth (and gums) exactly as you wish your child to brush.
4. Have your child brush exactly as you did. If your child makes any errors, correct them and have the child do it again.
5. If you use floss, do exactly the same thing with flossing (demonstrate, have the child do it correctly).
6. Demonstrate how to rinse and have your child do it after you.
7. Demonstrate how to clean up and put things away, then put things out again and have the child clean up.

Positive Practice. A *soft* child's toothbrush should be used for this so that the repeated practice will not irritate the child's mouth.

1. When you check the child and find that teeth are not brushed, make the child return to wherever the tooth brushing should have occurred.
2. Have the child go through the entire tooth-brushing routine.
3. Have the child put everything away and clean up.
4. Have the child return to wherever you checked his or her teeth.
5. Repeat procedures 1-4 five times. After each repeat check the child's mouth to make sure that gums are not being irritated. If this appears to be the case, do not give any more positive practice that day.

Menstruation: Sanitary Napkins and Tampons

Explicit teaching. In doing all aspects of explicit teaching related to menstruation you should stress that this is a normal function and shows that your girl is growing up.

1. If your child is not familiar with the normal physiological development which leads to the onset of menstruation, you should explain this in a matter-of-fact way before doing the remainder of explicit teaching on this topic. If you desire, you may get one of the pamphlets available from physicians, clinics, and some schools and libraries to help with this. Try to cover points 2-8 briefly and without awkwardness. Your child may say she is already familiar with these facts. Unless you are sure that she has accurate knowledge it would be wise to say that you would like to review these facts with her anyway.
2. Tell your girl that natural changes are taking place in her body which happen to every girl as she grows into an adult woman.
3. Tell her that inside her body is an organ called the uterus or womb.
4. Tell her that this organ is where babies grow if a woman becomes pregnant.
5. Tell her that *about* once a month, in a fully grown woman, cells grow in the uterus that help a baby develop if the woman is pregnant.

6. Tell your girl that if the woman is not pregnant, after a few days the body allows these cells to wash out of the body through the vagina. Tell her this is a normal process controlled by chemicals in the body called hormones.

7. Tell your girl that although part of this process involves blood washing out of the body, this bleeding is not a sign of sickness or injury but is actually a sign that her body is working in a normal, healthy fashion.

8. Explain to her that this is called menstruation. Tell her that at first it may not occur regularly as it does in a fully mature woman, and that sometimes it may be very slight, sometimes heavier. Make sure that she understands that these variations are normal.

9. Show her a sanitary napkin or tampon. Tell her that during menstrual periods these are used so that the material which normally is expelled will not stain clothing.

10. Explain exactly how she should use a sanitary napkin or tampon. You may wish to use the illustrations which are usually included with commercial products.

11. If you want, have her try using the product.

12. Explain when she should use a sanitary napkin or tampon, when they should be changed, how to dispose of them, and how long to use them.

13. Show her where the sanitary napkins or tampons are kept and stress that they will be there if she needs them. Tell her if she is unsure or wishes to check with you again, to be sure to ask.

14. Explain when she should carry sanitary napkins or tampons with her in case she needs them.

15. Ask if she has any further questions and answer any simply, honestly, and without embarrassment.

Positive practice. It is difficult for teenage girls to predict when a period will start. If a period starts and your girl has not used a sanitary napkin or tampon you should not count this as incorrect or make her do the positive practice. It is only an error if your girl has already noted that her period has started and does nothing about it, or if, after it starts, and she has already used a sanitary napkin or tampon, she forgets to do so later during the same period. In this case only, do the positive practice. In addition, you may not detect a failure until some time after the fact, perhaps when you sort clothing or do laundry. Thus the positive practice is somewhat different than for other grooming tasks and involves practice in correcting the problems caused by forgetfulness.

1. Collect all the clothes which have been soiled due to forgetfulness.
2. Tell your daughter calmly that she must have forgotten to use a sanitary napkin or tampon and will have to wash her clothes so that stains do not set.
3. Have your daughter rinse the clothes out in cold water to loosen stains.
4. If you use a stain remover spray or presoak, have your daughter do this.
5. Have your daughter wash, dry, fold, and put away the clothes.
6. There are no repeats for this positive practice.

Menstruation: Washing

You may wish to combine parts of this with the previous section on use of sanitary napkins and tampons.

Explicit teaching. Read procedures 1-8 in the section on sanitary napkins and tampons. You may wish to do these procedures before the explicit teaching on washing. You may wish to combine the two explicit teaching procedures into one if you feel both are necessary. If so, merely add the following steps on the end of the explicit teaching in the previous section.

1. Explain that to avoid soiling clothes or developing odor it is important that the girl do a thorough job of normal washing of her genital areas during a menstrual period.
2. State that this should include thorough soaping and rinsing of external parts of her genital area and vagina.
3. If you feel that due to discussion with other people, or due to advertising, your girl may feel that some douche, spray, or deodorant is necessary, you or she should check with a physician.
4. Make sure that your girl has no concerns that washing herself, along with whatever touching and handling is normally necessary in thorough washing, is harmful, or unhealthy. It is not.

Positive practice. Positive practice is done only when you have reason to believe that your girl bathed or showered after a menstrual period had started without correct washing of the genital area.

1. Have your girl go upstairs to the bath or shower and thoroughly wash the parts she missed.

2. If any clothes were soiled as a result, go through the same procedures as were described in the positive practice for use of sanitary napkins and tampons.

Menstruation: Not Cleaning After Accidents

Again, you may wish to combine the explicit teaching with the explicit teaching for the two previous sections. If so, add this on the end.

Explicit teaching. Go through each of the following steps with your girl.

1. Explain that sometimes a menstrual period may start unexpectedly and when a person is not prepared for it.
2. State that this may result in soiled clothes, legs, etc.
3. Say that sometimes this happens to everybody, and that it is noticeable only to the person it happens to unless they ignore it for hours.
4. Tell her that this is nothing to be embarrassed about and if it happens when she is at school or some other place she should ask permission to come home if that is necessary. Make sure that she understands that coming home is only necessary if she must change clothes or if washing is necessary and there are no provisions available. If all she needs is a sanitary napkin she can usually purchase one from a vending machine in most schools and public places and use it in the girls' room.
5. If she must change clothes or wash, tell her she should do the following:
   a. Wash thoroughly.
   b. Use a sanitary napkin or tampon.
   c. At home, rinse her clothes out in cold water and if necessary leave them to soak.
   d. Put on clean clothes.
6. Explain that problems can usually be avoided by keeping a few sanitary napkins or tampons in a place such as her purse, school bag, and school locker. Give her some for this purpose.

Positive practice. Positive practice is only done if your girl neglects to wash and change when it becomes necessary and is possible. An accident which is not avoidable and which is corrected when it later becomes possible to do so is not considered a failure in the grooming program. The positive practice is exactly the same as that for washing. Again, for health and practical reasons there is no repetition.

Wiping After Bowel Movements

Explicit teaching. Most adults expect young children to learn by themselves how to wipe themselves after a bowel movement, but if you wish your child to learn this quickly you must teach it.

1. Explain that after having a bowel movement (use your child's word) it is necessary to wipe correctly with toilet paper.
2. If your child asks why, explain that this will prevent the bottom from getting sore and keep underwear clean.
3. Take the child to the bathroom. Have him or her sit on the toilet or potty as if a bowel movement had just been completed.
4. Show your child exactly how much toilet paper to pull off. Also show your child how to fold it.
5. Although it is wasteful, for teaching purposes have your child practice tearing off the correct amount of paper and folding it, several times. Continue this until your child does it correctly with no trouble.
6. Explain how to wipe. If necessary, guide the child's hand.
7. Make sure the child holds the paper in a manner to prevent feces from getting on the hand.
8. It is considered better for girls to wipe by reaching behind their body and wiping with a movement from the front to the back. This prevents the small risk of a vaginal infection or irritation due to fecal material getting in the vagina.
9. Make sure that your child wipes gently, but firmly.
10. Explain that after wiping the child should look at the toilet paper and then drop it in the toilet. Tell your child that if the paper is not clean, he or she must wipe again. This should be done until the paper is clean after wiping.
11. Then have your child flush the toilet, dress, and wash the hands.
12. The next time your child has to have a bowel movement, tell the child to call you in to look at the last wipe so you can

see if the paper is clean. If it is not, point this out and have the child continue. When it is, repeat procedure 11.

13. If your child calls you in and shows you paper which is not clean, repeat procedure 12 with the next bowel movement and keep this up until he or she wipes adequately several times.

Positive practice. If, from checking, smell, or clothing, you note that your child has not wiped correctly, go through the positive practice. A problem caused by a child who has diarrhea or who is not completely toilet-trained is not considered an error in grooming. When you detect a failure, do the following:

1. Make the child go back to the bathroom, wipe until clean, flush, dress and wash, and return to you.
2. Make the child go back to the bathroom again, sit on the toilet again, wipe once lightly, dress, flush, wash, and return to you.
3. Repeat procedure 2 for a total of five times. Make sure the child wipes lightly "just to help remember" (to avoid an irritated, sore behind).

General Comments on Positive Practice

In the positive practice exercises it is important to avoid argument, confrontation, or any use of force. For this reason, the positive practice exercises are always given as an option; a child can regain a missed point by doing the positive practice required, but need not do so. If the child does not practice, he or she does not get credit that day.

Do not criticize the child for not performing the grooming task correctly the first time; merely note that it was not done and that if your son or daughter wants, the point can be regained by doing the positive practice exercise. Also do not criticize if he or she does not want to do the positive practice.

Provide praise for each step completed during a positive practice exercise, especially on those exercises which are repeated several times. Tell your child you are sure that it is unlikely that much forgetting will occur so he or she will not have to do positive practices often.

If your child regularly fails grooming tasks and does not do the positive practices, it probably means that the rewards are insufficient and that you are not giving enough praise for correct performances. Discuss this with your child and see if new or different rewards should be provided. If your child frequently fails a grooming task the first time, does the positive practices, and continues to make errors, you should repeat the explicit teaching several times.

It is also important to have as few grooming tasks on your list as possible. Aim for what is reasonable and what you can live comfortably with, not for perfection. The more tasks on the list the higher the possibility of failure will be, and you may end up spending an excessive amount of time doing positive practices. However, if you have only two or three tasks on your list, and do the explicit teaching carefully, you will probably rarely have to do a positive practice.

GOOD GROOMING LIST

Task	Mon.	Tues.	Wed.	Thurs.	Fri.	Sat.	Sun.	How Check	When
1									
2									
3									
4									
5									
6									
7									

THE GOOD KID BOOK

REWARD LIST

Reward	Points	Restrictions
1.		
2.		
3.		
4.		
5.		

GROOMING SUMMARY

Date	Grooming Tasks					Credit	Total	Spent	Balance
	1	2	3	4	5				

14.
Shouting, Tantrums, and Talking Back

WHEN a child shouts, talks back, or throws a tantrum it is usually pretty hard to take. Few adults enjoy it; few children like it very much, either. A house full of this sort of thing can make you wonder why you ever had children in the first place.

The great majority of behavior of this sort stems from three basic causes, none of which are very mysterious nor very specific to this set of problems. Let's make clear what these causes are:

- Shouting, tantrums, and loud talking back usually work. Few parents stick by their guns when subjected to this sort of on-slaught. Usually the child is not required to complete the chore requested, which led to the tantrum. If a child has been prohibited from doing something and then has a tantrum, the chances are the restrictions will not be enforced.
- Having a trantrum gets attention. If you don't think so, try it yourself!
- If other children or adults in the family shout, have trantrums, and talk back to each other, a child is likely to imitate it. This is especially true if a child sees that this behavior works for some-one else.

The solution to these problems is based on simple rules:

- Arrange things so tantrums, shouting and talking back do not work.
- Arrange things so that such behavior does not get attention.
- Remove models who shout, have tantrums, and talk back and whom your child may imitate.

Whom Is This Program For?

If your child is between ages four and about fifteen, and he or she has tantrums, shouts at you, or talks back strongly, this chapter may be appropriate. However, Chapter 4 is on whining, and you should refer to this if your child's behavior is mild enough to be called whining. If your child shouts and yells mainly with other children, you probably need to read Chapter 5 on fighting, arguing, and teasing. If, especially with an older child, occasional shouting or talking back is part of a general pattern of poor communications, you may find Chapter 16 more to the point. Glance through this and the other chapters before making a decision. After doing this, decide if this chapter is for you.

What Sets It Off?

There is usually more of a pattern to tantrums than most parents notice. Figuring out this pattern will make getting rid of the tantrums easier.

In the back of this chapter is the Tantrum Situations form. Its purpose is to help you discover if there are any particular situations which seem to precipitate tantrums (from here on, the word "tantrum" will also refer to fits of shouting and talking back, which are merely kinds of tantrums). Use it until you have recorded ten tantrums. Each time one of these incidents occur, fill in the form. Write down the date and time of occurrence in the first two columns. Under "Behavior" list what the child did. In the final column list the situation which led to the tantrum. Some typical ones might be:

- Told he cannot go out.
- Told she must go to bed.
- Asked to empty the garbage.
- Reminded he must clean his room before playing.
- Asked why he did not come home after school as told to.

To make this useful, there are two rules you must follow.

1. Accuracy and honesty. Make sure that you do not "revise" the situation so it will sound better. For instance, if you told a child that you would "beat the tar out of him" if he did not shape up and get out of the room at once, do not list as the situation that he had a tantrum when you would not allow him to stay

in the room. Record completely and accurately all that is pertinent, including your statement. If you asked your child to take out the dog and were ignored, and then you said, "You will have to go to bed thirty minutes early," at which point he had a tantrum, do not list the cause as "being asked to take out the dog." List the complete situation, and make clear what led to a tantrum.

2. Make sure you only record tantrums. Whining, saying "Do I have to," arguing, pouting, and sulking are not tantrums; screaming, yelling, shouting, and angry "backtalk" are. Record ten or more tantrums; then proceed to the next step.

Now you should find out if there is any pattern to the tantrums. To do this, look over the Tantrum Situations list and think about the following questions:

1. How many of the tantrums occurred when your child was asked to do some regular chore?

If five or more of the tantrums involved chores, I would suggest that you switch to Chapter 10, "Oh, Those Chores," and consider using that program instead of the one in this chapter.

2. How many of the tantrums occurred when you prohibited your child from doing something?

If five or more of the tantrums involved this situation, you may wish to consider the program in Chapter 1 on following directions, listed in the index, instead of this program.

3. How many of the tantrums followed your threatening the child with some sort of punishment?

If five or more of the tantrums were precipitated by threats, when you use this program pay special attention to the section on threats and promises.

4. How many of the tantrums occurred when you asked your child to do something which is not a regular chore?

If five or more of the tantrums started in this sort of situation, read the program in Chapter 1 on following directions and see if it seems appropriate.

If you have gotten this far and intend to use this program, you should read the rest of the entire chapter before continuing. After you have finished the chapter come back to the next section and start the program.

Threats and Promises

Most parents find it very difficult to handle problem behavior of children without using threats and promises. Threats are sometimes specific, e.g. "If you do not clean your room in ten minutes I'll spank you," and sometimes they are vague, e.g. "You'd better clean your room or you'll be sorry." Promises can be equally specific ("Clean your room and I'll let you watch TV") or vague ("You never know what good thing might happen if you clean your room up"). The use of frequent unsystematic threats and promises is usually undesirable. There are several reasons for this.

1. The chances are very high that you will be unable to fulfill more than a small proportion of such promises. This teaches your child that what you say is meaningless, and that consequences really do not follow behavior.

2. If you use a lot of random promises, and frequently do follow through, your child may learn to disobey you until you make some sort of promise of reward. In other words, the child will learn how to force you to offer a bribe, by disobeying when there is no bribe offered. If you occassionally reward your child for everyday good behavior, without promising anything in advance, the situation is different. Here, the child does not have to disobey to get you to promise a reward.

3. If you use a lot of threats, particularly vague threats, and follow through with them inconsistently, your child may learn to have tantrums or cry when you make a threat. This is because with most parents this will reduce the probability of the threat being carried out.

4. The use of threats and promises can cue your child to have a tantrum or to disobey. This is because most parents are likely to use a threat or a promise when they feel that the child is unlikely to obey without the threat or promise. Parents feel a child is unlikely to obey in situations in which the child has successfully disobeyed in the past. Sometimes parents use more threats or promises if they feel they are asking something unreasonable of a child. All of these factors may lead to a tantrum, since they are all signs that you are more likely to relent in this situation than in others. After all, if you were sure of yourself and felt

confident that your child would perform as requested, why would you use a threat or a promise?

You can see that it would be very helpful for you to cut down the number of threats and promises you make to your child. A reward or punishment which is actually given after good or bad behavior is not a threat or a promise—it is the real thing! Statements such as "That's what happens when you disobey (or obey)" accompanying an actual reward or punishment following behavior do not count as a threat or a promise.

To record your threats and promises, put a piece of masking tape or adhesive tape on your wrist each morning. It should be about three inches long and divided into two sections. One section should be marked "T" for threat, and the other should be marked "P" for promise. Throughout the day, each time you give a threat or a promise, mark an X on the tape to indicate that you have done so. In the illustration below we can see that Mrs. Smith made nine threats and seven promises during the day under consideration.

T	P
xxxxxxxxx	xxxxxxx

To help reduce the number of threats and promises you give, a six-day Threats and Promises chart is provided at the end of this chapter, along with a filled-out sample chart. The number of threats for each day is indicated by drawing a square around the number for that day. On Day 1 the mother made ten threats, and so she drew a square around the number 10 for Day 1. The number of promises is indicated by drawing a circle around the correct number of promises for that day. On Day 1 the mother made thirteen promises, so she drew a circle around the number 13 for Day 1. To help her see if her threats and promises were decreasing, she drew a graph through each of the days. This is shown on the sample. She connected all the threats (marked with squares) with solid lines, and all the promises (circles) with dotted lines. This helped her to see easily that although threats went up in Day 2, after that they decreased regularly. Promises decreased every day except from Day 3 to Day 4.

To see if you are using too many threats and promises, and to help you decrease them if you are, you should use the tape and the graph for six days. Go through the following steps each day:

1. Each morning put on the tape as illustrated.
2. Throughout the day, record threats and promises.
3. At the end of each day, mark your threats and promises for that day on the graph, using squares and circles.
4. Starting on Day 2, connect each day's square to the day before, using a solid line, and each day's circle to the circle to the day before, using a dotted line.

Try to get so you make five or fewer threats and five or fewer promises each day. If at the start you have fewer threats and promises than this, *and* if less than five of the tantrums recorded on the Tantrum Situation form were preceded by threats, you need not finish this exercise. However, if either of these conditions do not hold, you should. If you cannot get below six in the six days provided it would be wise to continue this procedure until you regularly can.

Bad Models

This section should be started at the same time as you are working on threats and promises. You need to do it only if you, other adults in the house, or other older children set a bad example by having tantrums, or shouting and yelling. If this is not a problem, skip this section.

As it is beyond the scope of this section to set up a formal program to change the behavior of several people in your family, the approach will be informal. Do the best you can—if you get some results it will make the rest of this program work a bit faster. If you do not get results, don't worry; things will just move slightly slower.

Get together with those people who you feel set bad examples which your child may be imitating. Without criticizing them or mentioning individual names, explain that you are starting a program to help your child have fewer temper tantrums, yell at you less frequently, and talk back less frequently. Merely say that you would appreciate it if other members of the family would try to cut down on this behavior so as to set a good example for the child in question. Make this low-key, and indicate that you will appreciate any help you can get.

Phase 1

In Phase 1 you start working with your child. The program is simple. You merely do the following:

1. The instant (not even three seconds later) that your child starts to have a tantrum, shout at you, or talk back loudly, turn around and go to another room. If it occurs outdoors, leave the area.
2. Do this every time this behavior occurs.
3. Make absolutely no comment at all.
4. In five minutes, return if you want. However, if after you leave you can hear the child continuing the tantrum, do not return until the tantrum has stopped for five minutes. If the tantrum started when you asked your child to do something, or told your child he or she could not do something, repeat the request or instruction in a matter-of-fact way as if nothing had happened when you return.
5. If another tantrum occurs, repeat the procedure exactly as you did the first time. In the beginning, you may have to do several repeats.
6. If your child makes any comment on your leaving when you return, merely say, "I don't have to listen to that."

Although the procedure is very simple, many parents find it difficult to carry through. You can do it, and after the first time or two it will become much easier. It is very important that you follow the six instructions exactly. You must never get into an argument or discussion with your child as a result of the tantrum, or of your leaving.

If your child merely raises an objection to what you have said, but does not have a tantrum, shout, or scream, do not carry out the procedure. Merely explain why this needs to be done or not done, or whatever is appropriate.

Many parents are surprised at how effective this approach is, particularly if all six steps are carried out exactly. It is important that if a request or an instruction you gave precipitated the tantrum, you repeat the request or instruction. Otherwise your child will learn that having a tantrum is effective.

During the five minutes that you are gone, you should fill out the Phase 1 Record. Record the date and time of the tantrum, and what started it. Check the six rules you should have followed; if you made any errors, list them. Leave the "Total for Day" section blank until your child has gone to bed. Then add up the total tantrums for that day, and enter this number in the box provided following the last tantrum for that day. Two of these forms are provided at the end of the chapter, and you can make more easily.

You are unlikely to see any improvement for about five days. Improvement can be noted by a reduction in the total tantrums per day on the record. Continue this procedure for two weeks. At that time, if your impressions are that things are definitely improving, and the record indicates the same thing, just continue this program until you feel it is not necessary any longer. If tantrums start again, start Phase 1 again.

If at the end of this time you do not see any improvement, start Phase 2.

Phase 2

Phase 2 is similar to Phase 1, except that instead of leaving yourself when a temper tantrum starts, you isolate the child. For instance, the minute a child starts a tantrum you may make the child go to the laundry room for five minutes. The exact requirements and details for this program will be spelled out.

To be able to carry out this program you must be able to meet the following criteria:

1. Some room in the house must be available which does not contain things to do in it which the child considers fun. There must be little to do or see there, and no toys or other things to provide amusement.
2. The child must be small enough or nonviolent enough so that when told to go to the room the child will go without a physical fight.
3. The child must be compliant enough so when sent or put in the room the child will stay until you give permission to leave. Some programs of this sort require locking a child in the room; such a program is best carried out only under professional supervision.
4. If the child is likely to have a tantrum in the room, to throw or break things, you must be able to prevent breakage.

If you can meet these criteria you can proceed with Phase 2 if Phase 1 was unsuccessful. If you cannot meet the criteria, do not use Phase 2. Instead, try Phase 1 for a longer period of time, look through other chapters in this book to see if there is one which may be more useful, or, if the problem is very serious, seek professional help from a child guidance or mental health clinic.

In preparation, select and prepare the room until it meets the requirements described above.

From here on, the program is similar to Phase 1. Here are the steps:

1. The instant (not even three seconds later) that your child starts to have a tantrum, shout at you, or talk back loudly, tell the child to go to the room or take the child to the room.
2. Make no other comment.
3. Do this every time the behavior occurs.
4. In five minutes (time it), let the child come out of the room. If after being placed in the room the child continues to have a tantrum, leave the child in the room until he or she has stopped for five minutes (time it). Mere talking, grumbling, etc. are not counted as tantrums.
5. If the tantrum started when you asked the child to do something or said the child could not do something, repeat the request or instruction in a matter of fact way when the child returns.
6. If another tantrum occurs, repeat the procedure exactly as you did the first time. In the beginning you may have several repeats.
7. If the child comments on the procedure, merely say, "If you are going to behave this way you will have to go to [name the room]."

The first few times you send the child to the room the child may continue to misbehave for some time. This should decrease after three or four experiences.

On the outside door of the room where you are to isolate the child, you should post the Phase 2 Record. This is the same as the Phase 1 Record with a few minor exceptions. Each time you place the child in the room you record the time, and also record the time when you let the child out. At the end of the day you not only record the number of tantrums, but the amount of time spent in the room. Keeping a record is very important for Phase 2.

Again, for the first few days you may not note any improvement. However, you should within a week. As this program is not meant to be cruel or harsh, you should follow these guidelines:

1. Ignore the first three days. However, after the first five days, if the child is spending over one hour a day in the room, discontinue the program and use one of the options suggested at the start of the Phase 2 description.

2. If the total daily time is averaging under one hour from Days 4 and 5 on, continue for two weeks. If you do not see a significant reduction in tantrums, and if your child frequently has to stay in the room for more than ten minutes at a time, discontinue the program and use one of the options mentioned.

3. If the program is relatively successful, based on your own impressions, few tantrums noted on the record, and only a small amount of time spent in the room, continue the program as long as you feel it is necessary. If problems recur, you may start it again.

You must keep the records correctly and regularly in Phase 2. If you are unwilling to do so, do not use the program.

Final Comments

Although the procedures described in this chapter are relatively simple, they are often difficult for parents to follow. In Phase 1 some parents find that they cannot help getting engaged in arguments or long verbal exchanges. The success of the program depends heavily upon your being able to avoid this. If you find it difficult, perhaps you can get a friend or your spouse or partner to monitor you.

Phase 2 is also difficult. On the one hand, we want to avoid setting up a program which is inhumane, either because it is not working, and thus serves no purpose, or because the child is spending an inordinate amount of time in isolation. On the other hand, children have usually learned that loud and long carrying-on will get them out of a variety of situations, and we do not wish to give into this when, in fact, given a few days the program will probably be successful. For these reasons specific guidelines for continuing or stopping were given. To follow these it is absolutely necessary that records be kept. If you do this, you should not have any serious problems.

Finally, make sure that this is the correct program for you to use. In several places in this chapter there are options discussed which may be more appropriate for your problem. Obviously, you want to use the easiest and most effective approach, so pay attention to these suggestions.

TANTRUM SITUATIONS

Date	Time	Behavior	Situation Leading To It

THE GOOD KID BOOK
SAMPLE

THREATS————————— AND PROMISES — — — —

Days 1	2	3	4	5	6
15	15	15	15	15	15
14	14	14	14	14	14
13	13	13	13	13	13
12	12	12	12	12	12
11	11	11	11	11	11
10	10	10	10	10	10
9	9	9	9	9	9
8	8	8	8	8	8
7	7	7	7	7	7
6	6	6	6	6	6
5	5	5	5	5	5
4	4	4	4	4	4
3	3	3	3	3	3
2	2	2	2	2	2
1	1	1	1	1	1

THREATS————————— AND PROMISES — — — —

Days 1	2	3	4	5	6
15	15	15	15	15	15
14	14	14	14	14	14
13	13	13	13	13	13
12	12	12	12	12	12
11	11	11	11	11	11
10	10	10	10	10	10
9	9	9	9	9	9
8	8	8	8	8	8
7	7	7	7	7	7
6	6	6	6	6	6
5	5	5	5	5	5
4	4	4	4	4	4
3	3	3	3	3	3
2	2	2	2	2	2
1	1	1	1	1	1

THREATS———————— AND PROMISES — — — —

Days 1	2	3	4	5	6
15	15	15	15	15	15
14	14	14	14	14	14
13	13	13	13	13	13
12	12	12	12	12	12
11	11	11	11	11	11
10	10	10	10	10	10
9	9	9	9	9	9
8	8	8	8	8	8
7	7	7	7	7	7
6	6	6	6	6	6
5	5	5	5	5	5
4	4	4	4	4	4
3	3	3	3	3	3
2	2	2	2	2	2
1	1	1	1	1	1

PHASE 1 RECORD

Date	Time	Cause of Tantrum	Errors	Total For Day

THE GOOD KID BOOK
PHASE 1 RECORD

Date	Time	Cause of Tantrum	Errors	Total For Day

PHASE 2 RECORD

Date	Cause of Tantrum	Time			Total Time in Room For Day	Total Tantrums For Day
		Put In	Let Out	Time in Room		

PHASE 2 RECORD

Date	Cause of Tantrum	Time			Total Time in Room For Day	Total Tantrums For Day
		Put In	Let Out	Time in Room		

15. Shyness

PARENTS are often upset about excessive shyness in children; everyone wants his child to get along well with others. Shyness frequently occurs in a child who does not seem to have any other problems, and though its causes may be mysterious, it is usually not difficult to correct. With such shy children what is needed is usually a little practice, teaching, and prompting, plus a small reward. If the teaching involves gradual steps with parental support, improvement can come quickly. This program will tell you how to help your child overcome shyness.

General Instructions

This simple program usually takes less than ten days. It requires a parent who is willing to spend close to ten hours over this period helping a child overcome shyness.

We have divided the social skills necessary for a child to introduce himself to other children into three separate types of behavior. After each step is taught and practiced at home, the parent helps the child to practice the new skills with other children. This procedure is then repeated for each of the skills. Finally, parental support is gradually eliminated.

In the beginning of this program, a lot of approval and candy rewards are used to help your child get started. As the program progresses, this is no longer necessary; the fun of playing with other children will be sufficient reward. No criticism or negative comments can be made for mistakes, balkiness, or shyness. You must never nag or threaten, and failures must be ignored. Much of the success of the program will depend upon your willingness and ability to do this. Remember, your child has already indicated that he or she is ill at ease in strange situations; negative experiences will only make this worse. Your job is to help your child have positive experiences in these situations.

The practice, both at home and in a natural play setting, is fairly structured at first. You will tell your child exactly how to act, bring the child to another child, and have your child do what you are teaching. Then you will remove your child, praise, and reward. Next, you will bring your child to another child and repeat the sequence. Sometimes, when you are teaching one type of behavior your child may spontaneously engage in play behavior which you have not yet taught. If this happens during a practice session, leave the children alone and allow things to occur naturally. After the play stops and your child is no longer interacting with the other child, remove your child, provide praise and a reward, and continue as if all your child had done was what you instructed. Teach later steps according to the program, even if the child has already engaged in these types of behavior. This will ensure that all necessary types of social behavior are well established.

There is a final thing to note before beginning. In this program you teach your child very specific things to say. At first your child may mimic these statements in a rote manner. Do not let this worry you; it is natural, to be expected, and it is temporary. As your child feels more at ease in these social situations you will note a large increase in spontaneity and creativity. Your child will soon start speaking in a normal conversational style. The natural interplay between children and the increasing confidence of your child will ensure this.

Situations

The teaching you do in this program occurs in two situations. You will have to arrange for these situations so they are available for you to use. The two situations are "at home" and "outside."

At home. The At-home situation is done in your own house or yard. It is a "role-playing" situation in which one, two, or three assistants are necessary. Your child should know the assistants and not be shy with them. The assistants can be children or adults; however, if they are adults they play the role of children and you always tell your child to pretend that they are unknown children. The assistants should be instructed to always behave in an ideal manner; that

is, if your child asks them a question, they should respond appropriately.

Outside. The outside practice is carried out in some natural play situation where there are several children, at least some of whom your child does not know. A park, playground, schoolyard, street, or yard where there are children is satisfactory.

Rewards

For the numbered types of behavior below, rewards are given every time your child performs correctly. Each reward will consist of praise for a good job, plus a small candy. Always give a reward for correct behavior. Please read the remainder of the program before starting.

Behavior 1: "Hi, what's your name?"

At home. Follow all the general instructions given previously. When you are all set, go through the following steps with your child and the assistants.

1. Have the assistants sit on the floor or grass and play as children your child's age might play.
2. Tell your child to pretend that these are unknown children playing.
3. Hold your child's hand. Walk up to one of the assistants and say to your child, "[Your child's name], say, 'Hi, what's your name?' "
4. If your child does not say, "Hi, what's your name?" prompt your child again, saying that it is just a game.
5. The minute your child does say this, lead him or her away from the assistants, and give praise and a candy. Then say, "Let's do it again."
6. Repeat Steps 3-5 at least fifteen times. If your child does not do this easily and without hesitating at the end of fifteen times, continue it longer until the child does.
7. At the end tell your child that you will practice this with some real children later.

Outside. Later the same day, preferably when your child is somewhat hungry and again interested in candy, take the child to the "outside" location where several children, not all of whom your child knows, are playing. In the outside situation go through Steps 3-6 of the "at-home" portion, this time with real children. At the end, tell your child what a very good job the child did and how much fun it was.

If your child has troubles with the outside practice, repeat the at-home practice and the outside practice the next day. Continue this until it is no longer a problem.

In this outside practice, and in all outside practices which follow, a difficulty may arise when some other child refuses to respond or responds in an inappropriate way. If this occurs, quickly move your child to a new child, saying, "Let's try someone else," and repeat the instruction at once.

Behavior 2: "My name is so and so."

In this part you teach your child to tell his or her own name after asking for the other child's name.

At home. After everything is set up, tell your child he or she is going to learn some more about playing.

1. Practice Behavior 1 ("Hi, what's your name?") twice, with lots of approval and occasional candy. If there is any problem, practice it longer.
2. Then, after an assistant responds to your child by giving his (the assistant's) name, tell you child to say, "My name's so and so." (Use child's name.)
3. Repeat Step 2 about ten times. Each time, make sure that your child asks the other child's name, and, after being told, responds by giving his or her own name. Remind the child to do the second part if necessary. Also prompt the first part if necessary.
4. At this point your child may start telling the other child his or her name spontaneously after hearing the other child's name. If so, reward at the end of both exchanges. If your child does not start spontaneously giving his or her name after the assistant gives his name, change your initial instruction to "Say, 'Hi, what's your name?' and when they tell you, say, 'My name is so and so (child's name)'!"
   In other words, now you give your child instructions to make both responses all at once as you lead your child up to an assistant.
5. If your child occasionally fails to make either response, repeat the necessary part of the instruction at the time the child fails to make the correct response.

6. Repeat this procedure until your child asks for the other child's name and then without reminders gives his or her own name ten times. In other words, at this point, when you say, "Say, 'Hi, what's your name?' and when they tell you say, 'My name is so and so (child's name)'," your child should go up to an assistant, ask the assistant's name, and then tell the assistant his or her own name with no further instructions.

Remember, after each successful performance you praise your child and give a candy. As the child gets the knack, give candy only occasionally.

7. Now repeat Step 6, except as you lead your child to the assistant say, "Introduce yourself," and *then* give the instruction as in Step 6. Repeat this until you have ten successful trials.
8. Now repeat Step 7, except *only* say, "Introduce yourself." Give your child a reminder only if asking the other child's name, or giving his or her own name, is omitted. Continue this until ten times in a row on the instruction "Introduce yourself" alone your child asks what the assistant's name is and after hearing it gives his or her name.

Again, remember to praise each success with approval and occasional candy.

Outside. Go through Step 8 with real children. If your child has a problem, start with Step 7, and when your child is successful with Step 7 ten times in a row go to step 8. Repeat Step 8 until you have ten successes in a row.

Behavior 3: "Can I play?"

In this part, you teach your child to say, "Can I play?" after he or she has gone through the introductions.

At home. This is started the same as for the previous types of behavior.

1. Practice the final performance for behavior two several times.
2. After several successes, after your child gives his or her name, say, "Say, can I play?"
3. Repeat Step 2 above several times. If your child has any problems with this, indicate what should be said. Continue until your child has ten successes, giving a correct introduction and then on your instruction saying, "Can I play?"

Remember to continue to reward correct performances with occasional candy and regular approval.

4. This time, when you lead your child to an assistant, say, "Introduce yourself and then ask if you can play." If your child omits any part of the routine, prompt him or her to make all three utterances (asking for other child's name, giving own name, asking to play).

5. Continue Step 4 until your child goes through the introduction and asking to play with an instruction from you only at the beginning, ten times in a row.

6. Change your instruction to the following: "Play with those children. Introduce yourself and ask if you can play."

7. If your child leaves out any step (asking name, giving name, asking if he or she can play), prompt the child.

8. Continue this until you have ten successes.

9. Change your instruction to the following alone: "Play with those children."

10. If your child leaves out anything (asking name, giving name, asking to play), prompt the child. Continue this until you have ten successes with only the instruction "Play with those children."

Remember to praise and reward successes with occasional candy.

Outside. Repeat Step 10 of the at-home practice with real children until you have about fifteen successes. Remember to praise regularly and use candy rewards once in a while. You may also wish to give candy to the children your child plays with.

If your child has a problem doing this, start with Step 6 of the at-home practice. After several successes, move ahead, using Step 10 of the at-home practice.

Ending: You Get Out of the Picture

This is the only part which does not have an at-home section; all of it is done with children in an outside situation.

1. Take your child out to where children are playing and go through the final performance of Behavior 3 a few times, perhaps until you have two or three successes. Reward all successes.

2. Repeat several more times, only omit the candy. Still praise.

3. Repeat several more times. Praise only about one-third of the time. Do not give any candy.

After the play session is over, tell your child how well the child played and give a candy.

4. Take your child outside to play on another occasion. When you get close to other children, just say, "Go and play now." If your child seems hesitant, merely say, "You know what to do."
5. As your child plays, occasionally make remarks to the entire group of children such as "My, you're having fun!" or "You kids know how to play" or "What good children you are."

After you make such a remark, stroll off so that your child will not stop playing to look at you or talk with you. After play sessions talk with your child about what things your child and the other children did and how much fun it seemed to be.

In subsequent play sessions, do not stay near the playing children, but walk off and come back occasionally to make remarks about the play. Continue this until your child seems at ease with you absent, and then gradually start doing whatever you would normally do while the children play.

Final Comments

In this program you have taught your child some basic social skills by instructing very specifically in small steps. You rewarded success and when your child failed to make a correct response you prompted the correct response, and then gradually stopped prompting. If your experience is typical of most, you probably found that the normal fun of playing gradually affected your child and that your guidance and support were no longer necessary. Too often we assume children learn naturally without any teaching. A little direct teaching can often smooth out what may otherwise become a more serious problem.

16.
My Child Never Tells Me Anything

PARENTS and children—particularly teenagers—often have difficulty talking to each other. A great deal has been written about this, and it certainly deserves attention. Usually, communications improve when specific problems are solved; an angry, nagging, bickering relationship does not promote free and open talk. If you have successfully used any of the procedures in this book it is likely that you already communicate more easily with your children. The material in this chapter focuses on several specific skills which I have found are important when communication is a problem. Although the emphasis is on adolescents, the approach is useful with other children as well.

Overview

Probably the most common barrier to free and open communication is that adolescents are frequently punished for talking with their parents. Sometimes this is quite obvious, sometimes it is subtle. Usually it is unintentional. Look at the following illustrations.

Mother: Where did you go after school?
John: Oh, a couple of us went over to Brad's to listen to records.
Mother: Was Milt [another adolescent the parent feels is a "bad" influence] there?

The first reaction of John's mother to his statement was a subtly punishing remark; his mother was checking up on him. Let's take another example.

Frank: Boy, after school today we really had a wild time at Stanley's.

Father: I thought you said you had a lot of homework this week.

Here, instead of responding to his son's statement, Frank's father immediately, if subtly, criticized the boy for not doing homework. The actual content of Frank's remark was ignored. Here's a third.

Parent: How's your job going?

Mary: Oh, I don't know, it's really getting to be a drag—I've been thinking of quitting.

Parent: Can't you stick at anything for over a week?

In this case Mary started to tell her parent about job difficulties, but was immediately punished for irresponsibility without being allowed to describe the situation. Let's look at a fourth.

Mother: What happened at the dance last night?

Alice: It was really strange. A bunch of guys came in who were drunk or stoned and started making a big—

Mother: That's why I don't like you going to that place.

Note that Alice did not say she was involved in these activities. She was being honest and open with her mother, who immediately punished her for talking freely. In similar circumstances in the future Alice will probably say, "Oh, nothing."

Father: Why were you so late last night?

Carlos: Well, I don't know how to tell you this . . . but I had a slight accident with Bob's car.

Father: That's why I didn't want you to drive! You're so careless. What happened?

Even if Carlos is a careless driver, his father has punished him for telling about what happened, not for poor driving. It would be more sensible to reward Carlos for being honest about what happened and handle the driving in some other way.

Parents often expect or at least are worried about a variety of possible troubles with adolescents. Sometimes this is based on experience, sometimes it is not. In either case it may result in being punishing, critical, or negatively inquisitive when talking with adolescent children; the child is punished for talking about anything other than trivialities.

In addition, adults often find it difficult to treat adolescent problems seriously. When an adolescent starts to discuss something and is brushed aside or made to feel that a parent does not have time to talk,

the adolescent's conclusion is that the parent does not consider things in his or her life significant. Adults often brush off the problems of adolescents by telling them it is "just a stage" or "you will grow out of it" or it is "normal" and "happens to everybody." While very few of us have unique problems, being told it is "normal" or a "stage" or that "everybody has had that problem" hardly helps us solve it. Few of us like to discuss our problems with a person who treats casually what we find important.

Serious talk between parents and pre-adolescent children is usually one-sided. On serious topics, the parents talk and the children listen. When this carries over into adolescence it reduces communication. In addition, parents rarely talk to young children or adolescents on serious topics relating to the parents. The concerns and worries of parents are usually seen as topics to be talked about with other adults. A person is more likely to discuss his or her personal life with those who talk to themselves about their personal life. A parent who never talks to children about things important to the parent may find that the children do not talk about things important to them.

In an attempt to set a good example for children, many adults talk to adolescents without ever admitting their own weaknesses, errors, and areas of uncertainty. Children often feel that adults act as if they have no questions, and as if they know for sure that certain things are unalterably bad and others are always good. Adolescents may interpret ideal goals set by adults as realistic expectations for everyday behavior. Parents seen as holding such views may be seen as incapable of understanding the ambiguities, failures, and unsureness which adolescents experience.

Fortunately, communications can be opened up between parents and their adolescent children by reducing the subtle punishment given adolescents for talking, by taking them seriously, by talking more openly to them about important things, and by being more honest about human failings. In exchange you will find it easier to influence your adolescent.

How to Begin

Read the entire program before doing anything. If you have a spouse or partner you should both read the program before beginning. Discuss it and make sure you both understand what it is about and agree on how to do it. Then return to the section which follows and start the program.

Where Do We Stand?

A good way to start a program to improve something is to assess how things are now. The procedure involves getting information on the current general status of communications between you and your adolescent(s), as well as information on three specific areas. These areas are:

1. *Criticalness.* This determines whether people feel that communicating is punished.
2. *Being taken seriously.* This covers whether your adolescents feel you take them seriously, and includes information on whether they feel you take time to listen to them, treat what they say as important, and talk to them about serious things.
3. *Standards.* This covers whether your children feel you have reasonable and realistic standards for them, whether you apply these fairly to them as well as to yourself, and whether they are concerned over not living up to your standards.

A Parent-Adolescent Communication Scale (PACS) is included at the end of the chapter. The child should fill one out; if you have more than one child make a copy for each. Also make a copy for each parent. Parents should rate themselves as they believe the child might. Make sure that each person filling out a PACS form reads the instructions.

Go over each child's PACS form with him or her. There are no right or wrong answers, or secret meanings to interpret. The guide which follows may help you.

General Communications section. Questions 1 and 2 are overall ratings of how good communications appear to be. The more the ratings are to the left, the better your child feels communications are. Scores in the right-hand half suggest that your child would like more or better communications. A rating near the left on Question 3 may mean that your child feels that communications are satisfactory. However, it may also mean that the individual feels there is little communication, but does not want any more. You will have to ask your adolescent to explain this. The same possibilities exist for Question 4.

Criticalness. This section is meant to help you assess whether your adolescents feel that they don't talk freely because they fear punishment. Scores to the left on Questions 5 through 10 suggest that they do not feel you are overcritical when they talk to you, while scores to the right suggest a concern over this. Scores to the right on Questions 11 and 12 suggest that your children would like more communications but that fear of punishment prohibits this; they may mean also that you are not critical now, so being less critical would not improve things. You will have to ask them to explain these two scales.

Being Taken Seriously. Scores to the left indicate that your adolescents feel that you take their ideas, problems, and concerns seriously. Scores in the right half suggest they feel that there is some problem in this area.

Standards. Scores to the left on Questions 18 through 23 indicate that your adolescents feel you are fair, reasonable, and are not hypocritical concerning standards, morality, and judgments. Scores to the right suggest that they feel there are problems in this area which retard communication.

Finally, go over anything listed for Question 24.

Now, with your children, you should go over the PACS on which you rated yourself. The main value of this is noting areas where you and your children disagree. It is probably correct to assume that on any question where you and your children have a rating difference of more than about one-third of the scale, there is a difference in perception worth discussing. If you saw a problem on an item and they did not, circle the item on your form. Explain to them the reasons you felt this area was a problem. Ask them to explain why they did not. Discuss the item until the reason for the disagreement is clear.

Put an asterisk on your PACS before items where your children saw a problem and you did not. Again, discuss these items until you feel sure that you understand the disagreement.

In going over the PACS you must not argue or try to make people defend their points of view. Everyone is merely stating how he or she feels, and no one else can argue about this. Each person is the authority on how he or she feels. The goal is to find out these feelings, and to see where there are problems or disagreements.

Fill out the PACS Summary which follows. This is merely a way of putting the information from the PACS forms into a more concise arrangement. The instructions on it are self-explanatory. You can use it to stress or omit certain parts of the programs which follow, depending upon their importance.

Reducing Punishment and Criticism for Communicating

If the PACS Summary suggested that either general communications or criticalness were problems, it is important that you complete this part of the program. If these areas were not suggested as problems, it may not be useful to complete this section. Look over your PACS Summary and read the section. Then make a decision as to whether you will go through these procedures.

There are two parts to this program. The first consists of exercises to role-play with your children. The second is a program to carry out in daily life after you have completed the role-playing.

Role-Playing

This part should be done only if your children are cooperative. If, after you explain it, they refuse to do it, skip it and go directly to the next part. In the first step you assess whether or not they are willing to participate.

Rationale and preparation. The goal of this exercise is to help you feel at ease, and be noncritical, when your adolescents tell you things which disturb you. You want to encourage them to tell you about things by not punishing them or criticizing them for talking to you. If they bring up things which you feel you need to pursue, after you have gotten the full picture you can discuss issues that concern you with them in a nonpunitive manner, treating these concerns as a mutual problem, rather than as something they have done "wrong."

In the role-playing your children will make up things to tell you about themselves, their activities, or their friends, which they assume would, if real, be very upsetting. Sometimes they may just hint at these things, to see if you will "come down" on them if they go into further detail. Your job will be to avoid any punishing statements, statements of a critical nature, statements which imply that you are unhappy with them, or statements which suggest that you feel that they have probably done lots of other horrible things which they do not wish to tell you about. Your job also will be to reward them for talking openly to you and make clear that you are pleased that they feel able to talk about such things with you, without suggesting that you condone all the things they have told you about.

Before starting, you must explain what you want to do to your children. Tell them you want to learn how to listen to them better, and to listen without being critical. Tell them that you want to practice communicating openly with them, even about things which might disturb you. Tell them that their job will be to make up things to tell you which they think would disturb you if real, and that you will try to respond to them without being negative. Explain that it is just role-playing, that they can make up anything they want, and that you want them to tell you if you say something which in a real situation would discourage them from talking further. Explain each step to them in advance.

Preparation of stories. At the end of this chapter is the Story Checklist. Give it to your children. Tell them they are to make up one situation from each category which they are going to tell you about as if it were real. Their job will be to take each story and start telling you about it as an adolescent might start talking about such a topic to a parent. They are to tell you how well you encourage them to keep talking, and what you do that discourages further talking. In this step they are to make up the stories which they will later tell you, using the checklist.

Scheduling. Set up four thirty-minute sessions with your adolescents. During each of these sessions you will role-play a conversation in which they tell you one of the stories they have made up and you will try to respond in a manner that encourages communications.

Session 1. In Session 1, the types of remarks you are to make are very restricted. You can only say things which reward talking, but cannot ask questions or make comments. Statements such as the following are acceptable:

Uh huh.
I see.
OK.
Tell me.
That's interesting.
Tell me more about it.
I don't understand, explain again.

Session 2. In Session 2 you can make remarks such as those you made in Session 1, as well as remarks which make some statement about how you feel your child must have felt in the "situation." In addition to the types of remarks made in session one you can say things such as:

You must have felt embarrassed.
That must have been frightening.
That sounds like it was funny.

Questions of the same sort are also acceptable, such as:

Was it scary?
Did you feel helpless?
I would have gotten angry—did you?

To make realistic responses of this sort will require that you really listen to what your children are saying. As you listen, try to imagine how the person speaking must have felt in the situation. Listen for statements of the following kind and respond with appropriate remarks.

1. Speaker explicitly states feeling; you respond with a restatement. *Example.* Child: "It was frightening." You: "I can see how you would be really scared."
2. Speaker uses emotional tone of voice but does not state feeling; you ask about feeling. *Example.* Child: "That just wouldn't work." You: "Were you frustrated?"
3. Speaker states situation that must have been emotional, but does not state emotion; you mention feeling as statement or question. *Example.* Child: "No matter what I said nobody would listen." You: "That must have been annoying."

Session 3. In this session you can make all the types of remarks you made in the first two sessions, plus asking noncritical questions to get further information. You must be very careful to make sure that such remarks are not subtle criticism. For instance, if your child has just described a situation in which another child made a derogatory remark about your child's sister, and you then ask, "What did you say?" it may just be a chance to get further information. But it also could be said in a way and in a context which implies that the child should have done something, and you are checking up to see if he did. Only neutral questions to get information are acceptable. Ask your children if your questions come across this way.

Session 4. In this last session you can make all the types of statements you made in previous sessions. However, in this session you also bring up matters which concern you. For instance, if in this exercise your son were to describe an incident relating to driving an automobile which you felt was dangerous and indicated bad judgment you would discuss those concerns. However, the manner in which this is done is very important as far as maintaining good future communications. There are three rules you should follow:

1. *Timing.* When in the conversation you bring up your concerns is very important. The main idea is that you should not interrupt what you are being told to express your concerns, but should bring up your concerns after your son or daughter has told you the entire incident. There are several reasons for this. The first is that interruping the minute a possibly dangerous, unwise, or questionable item is mentioned punishes further talking. Second, it suggests that you are only interested in finding out "bad" things. It suggests that you are not interested in what your children have to say, and assume that they have nothing to add which may throw further light on the incident, how they handled it, or their opinion or analysis. So the first rule is to not bring up such concerns until your children have finished saying what they have to say on that topic.

2. *Criticism.* The second rule is that you should not bring something up in a critical manner. Do not make negative remarks about the child, but comment factually on the situation. Here are some examples:

   Good: It seems that letting an unlicensed person drive your car could get you all in legal trouble, or lead to an accident.

   Bad: Letting someone unlicensed drive your car is really stupid; you could get fined or have an accident.

   Good: If someone hangs around with a person who sells drugs other people may assume that they are involved in this sort of stuff.

   Bad: Only an idiot would hang around with someone like that and chance ruining his reputation.

3. *Emotion.* If the situation is one about which you feel emotional, state how it makes you feel, not your reaction to your son or daughter or how they are responsible for the emotion. Here are some examples:

   Good: I get really worried when I think of you in situations like that.

   Bad: You're always doing things that make me worry about you.

   Good: I always get upset when I hear about that group.

   Bad: When you are with those people I always expect the worst.

Most of the time, you should use the word "I" to stress how you feel and avoid the word "you" or your child's name in describing your reaction. Describe your reaction, not what they did.

Discussion. After Session 4, discuss the sessions with your children. Get them to tell you how the way you handled the discussions affected them. Ask them to try and describe anything you did which is different from most discussions you have on similar (real) topics and whether your changes in handling these things made it easier for them to talk to you.

Everyday Situations

You can now go on using this approach in everyday situations. It will have a more rapid effect if you were able to do the role-playing, but over time should work in any case. Here is a summary of some of the things you should do when your adolescents talk with you:

- *Listen.* Take the time to listen to them.
- *Reward talking.* Make general remarks, as you did in session one, which reward talking and indicate that you are listening and interested.
- *Reflect feelings.* As was described for session two, restate feelings expressed. This will ensure that you understand what is important to them and will make this clear to your children.
- *Question.* Ask noncritical questions, as was described for session three, to get the information you need to understand what they are telling you.
- *Express concerns.* Express your concerns, waiting until the appropriate time, being noncritical, and expressing how *you* feel.

There is no time limit for how long you should do this; if you wish to maintain open communications these are things you should always do. Obviously, in an actual conversation you will have things to say which go beyond those things suggested in the role-playing. For instance, you may describe your experience, provide information, or discuss complications or consequences of some action. However, although you will need to do all these things you should not do anything which contradicts these guidelines.

Taking Adolescents Seriously

Your child will not talk to you about serious things if it appears that you consider them trivial. Many of the things you have done in the earlier parts of this chapter will help dispel the idea that you see your son's or daughter's concerns as unimportant. Here are some additional ideas on this topic.

Having time. In the early evening before or after dinner many adults feel very rushed with household chores or things they have hoped to get done all day. In addition, at this time it is natural to be preoccupied with things which have happened during the day. However, this is the time most children find appropriate to talk over things with their parents which have come up during the day. Frequently, parents do not realize that they discourage this sort of talk with comments such as "Let me finish the paper first" or "Could we talk later —I'm really tired now," or by simply not paying attention. If you wish to encourage your children to talk you have to be available when things are bothering them. When you are approached, if it is at all possible, you should stop what you are doing and give your full attention to the conversation at hand. If this is impossible, make clear that you do want to hear about the topic and that you will have time a bit later. Tell your child you will talk when you finish what you are doing, and then make sure that you do.

For five days make a determined effort to go out of your way to have time when your children attempt to talk with you. Note the reaction to this carefully.

It happens to everybody. Many adolescents have problems with school or a job, or trouble with a boyfriend or girlfriend, or have acne or problems over things like shyness. That the problems are common or that they will be outgrown does not make them any less painful. In general, avoid making remarks such as "Everybody goes through that" or "It's natural at your age" or "It's just a stage" or "You'll outgrow it." In most cases such remarks sound as if you are writing off the problem as very minor. However, when there is a concern over being unusual, such remarks should be made in a reassuring way that does not sound as if you consider the problem itself inconsequential. Other than for reassurance do not make this kind of statement.

Serious talk. Many adults "protect" their children from serious topics. Certainly, there are some things which it would be unwise to discuss with your children under certain circumstances. Obviously, there are more things you would discuss with an older child than with a younger child. For instance, personal problems between parents may be a private matter. However, if these get to a point where they are affecting a child's life or will lead to a major change in a child's life, such as a divorce, it is foolish not to talk these over in general terms with an older child. They are probably aware of the problem anyway and will eventually find out about it, so talking it over may help prepare them or reassure them that the problem is not with them.

Many important family topics, however, will have a definite effect on a child. Things such as a possible move, a possible job change, or a change in financial status will change a child's life, and a child should be told about these things, especially an adolescent. Talking such things over may provide you with important information useful in making a decision, will indicate that you respect the opinions of your adolescent, and will help your children and you to prepare for the possible change.

Parents also frequently "protect" their children from knowledge of temporary daily things which have importance only in the short run. For instance, if one parent is quite upset over having too much to do at work there are many benefits from casually letting children know this, much as you would an adult. Given a reason for your mood, they may be less disturbed by it. If your children are more aware that you are human and have problems, they may discuss their problems more freely with you.

At the end of this chapter is an Important Family Matters form. Spend a few minutes thinking about significant things which will affect your family. In each box under "Topic" list one of these, using some short word or discription. In the "Informed" column write down "Yes" or "No" depending upon whether the children are informed on this topic. Then think about each topic, and make a decision as to whether or not there are good reasons not to inform the children. If there are, write "Yes," and if not, write "No." Circle topics about which you have not informed the children, indicated by "No" in the "Informed" column and for which you also wrote "No" in the "Reason Not To" column. These circled topics are items which you feel your children might hear about, but which you have not yet discussed with them.

Based upon the form, pick one topic which you have not discussed with your children to date, but which you would like to talk about. Find a convenient time to talk and tell your children that you want to talk about something which you feel is important. Then tell them:

1. What the issue and the facts are.
2. Why you feel it is important.
3. What consequences this might have.

Using the approaches discussed earlier, ask your children to give their opinions.

Do not be surprised if what you felt was an important topic is seen as uninteresting by your adolescents. Just as parents sometimes react this way to their children, chilen often react this way to parents. Even if this is the case, the fact that you have clearly indicated its importance to you, and have then discussed it, should have a good effect.

Depending upon your estimate of the first discussion of important family topics, you may wish to also discuss other similar topics from the form. This is a matter you will have to decide. If you decide to discuss additional topics and if these topics are what you might call "bad news," spread the discussions out over several weeks and re-strict them to things that are of importance to your children and that they have a right or a need to know. The goal is not to unload a lot of problems on your children. Use your judgment.

Standards. A friend of mine once told me that ideally he would like his children to get all As in school. Given what his son had been doing in the past year he said that a realistic goal would be for his son to get a low B average. Finally, he said that he would not be upset as long as his son did not flunk anything. This would be minimally acceptable.

The difference between what we consider ideal, a realistic goal, and an acceptable level of accomplishment is important. Many times parents communicate an ideal level of performance to their children as if it is a goal or what is minimally acceptable. An ideal is some-thing we strive toward but rarely achieve. If a child believes that your ideal is actually a goal or a minimally acceptable performance, it will seem as if it is impossible to please you. It will also seem as if you are unrealistic and ignorant of the imperfections of human beings. This will make it appear that you will be displeased with anything honest told to you, and will result in your not being told very much. Children may also assume that you do not "practice what you preach," as it is unlikely that you do everything "ideally," unless you are very exceptional.

It is therefore important to communicate to your children the difference between what you would ideally like to see, what you feel is a realistic goal, and what is minimally acceptable, both in matters concerning your children and in those concerning yourself. To help you clear up your ideas concerning ideals, goals, and acceptable behavior, two forms are provided. One is My Ideals for Myself, and the other is My Ideals for My Children. It would be very difficult to fill these out for every area of life; fill them out for areas which you feel are of current concern or confusion between you and your children.

My Ideals for Myself. On this form you are concerned only with ideals that directly affect or influence your communication with your children. For instance, do you suggest to your son or daughter that getting angry or losing one's temper is unforgivable, but get angry yourself and lose your own temper on occasion? Do you preach that if a job is worth doing it is worth doing well, but frequently do less than your best? Do you tell your children that it is always bad to lie, but occasionally get caught in a fib yourself? Do you say that it is very bad to make snap decisions, yet let your children see you decide things on the spur of the moment? These are things we all do. Nobody but you (and perhaps your children) can tell you which areas are important here. Spend some time thinking about this, make some notes, and discuss it with your spouse or partner before filling out the form. Then list topics of concern.

The next part of each section of the form concerns the ideal. List here what you believe is the ideal for each area you have decided is important. In the second section, instead of the ideal, list what is a realistic goal for this area. In the final section list what you feel is the minimally acceptable way to behave in this area. Do this for each topic you have decided is important. To help you, here are some illustrations to give you some ideas of how to use the form.

Topic	Ideal	Goal	Acceptable
Lying	I never lie.	I only lie when it is for someone else's good, or little white lies.	I may lie sometimes, but never maliciously or to hurt someone.
Work	I always do my best.	I do at least as well as others expect.	I do things well enough to get by.

Topic	Ideal	Goal	Acceptable
Helping	I always help others when needed, whether or not I am asked.	I help others when asked, if possible.	I can be counted on by close friends in an emergency.
Family	I always do what is best for the family.	Sometimes I put my own needs ahead of the family, but not in serious matters.	I never intentionally do things to hurt the family, but sometimes do due to thoughtlessness.

It does not matter how world-shaking or trivial your topics appear. All that is important is that you include those you feel are significant now. Collect your notes, ideas, etc., and try filling out the form.

My Ideals for My Children. Now you must do the same thing for topics related to your children. On this you fill in what you feel are ideal ways of behaving, realistic goals, and acceptable minimums for your children. Again, collect your ideas first and only fill in topics which are currently areas of disagreement, unsatisfactory performance or some sort of issue. Some things you list may be general topics, many or all may be very specific. Use a different form for each child. In filling this form in, remember your experience in filling out your own form. Be realistic concerning goals and what is minimally acceptable.

Using these forms. If the PACS indicated problems in the area of "Standards," communications with your children will be aided by formally going over what you have discovered filling out these two forms. If Questions 18, 19, and 20 on the PACS were rated far to the right, it suggests that your children feel you do not practice what you preach. Discussion with them of the difference between ideals, goals and acceptable standards on the form you filled out on your own ideals may help clear up this area. Problems indicated on Questions 21, 22, or 23 of the PACS should be helped by discussing the form you filled out for your children. In your discussion make clear that you would really like it if the "goals" were reached, but will be severely disappointed only by behavior below the "acceptable" level.

Further use of the forms. The suggestions for further use of these forms are very general. In everyday conversation make sure that you clarify the difference between the different levels of expectation. For instance, if you find out that your child has told a lie, and if you agree with the sample form given earlier, do not say, "You should never lie—I never do," but say, "You should try not to lie, although I realize sometimes we do lie under pressure or to avoid hurting someone. Tell me what happened."

Final Comments

Communications problems are rather complex, and somewhat more difficult to correct than many of the problems discussed in other chapters. A standard step-by-step program is also less appropriate for correcting communications difficulties than for some other topics in this book. This chapter has presented a series of suggestions for improving communications, particularly with adolescents, based upon the most typical issues which cause problems. Many of the suggestions require some reorientation or exploration of personal beliefs and modes of operation on your part. I hope that most of the suggestions fit in with your style and ideas.

Conflict, troubles of some sort, and disagreements are typical in families with adolescents. It may be futile to hope that no conflicts will arise; a more realistic goal may be to hope that when problems do arise they can be discussed and defused.

_____   _____
(NAME)   (PERSON RATED)

PARENT-ADOLESCENT COMMUNICATION SCALE

INSTRUCTIONS

This rating is *not* designed to determine how well or how poorly your parents are doing. It is also not designed to compare your parents with any other adults, or to rate your parents in terms of some standards as to how parents should act. It is solely for the purpose of stating how things are going in terms of how you feel and how you would like them to be. Its purpose is to help you and your parents make any changes you both feel would make life better. Make each rating honestly. You will have a chance to discuss this with your parents and to explain more specifically any items you wish to. Place an "X" on each scale at the point that best expresses your feeling. If you wish, you may place an X to indicate how an item applies to your father, and an O for how it applies to your mother.

GENERAL COMMUNICATIONS

1. Regardless of what is said, do you feel you and your parents communicate as much as you would like?

   |_____|_____|_____|_____|
   As much   Somewhat   Much too
   as I want   little

2. Do you feel that the communications you do have with your parents are easy, open, and straightforward?

   |_____|_____|_____|_____|
   Definitely   Somewhat   Would like
   yes   improvement

3. Do you feel you talk to your parents as much as you would like?

   |_____|_____|_____|_____|
   Definitely   Somewhat   Definitely
   yes   no

4. Do you feel your parents talk to you as much as you would like?

Definitely   Somewhat   Would like
yes   improvement

CRITICALNESS

5. When you talk to your parents about things you do, do you feel that they are looking for "bad" things or criticize you frequently, whether on purpose or accidentally?

Never   Sometimes   Often

6. When you talk to your parents, do you feel that they assume you may have done something they disapprove of?

Never   Sometimes   Often

7. When you talk to your parents do you feel it is necessary to avoid topics so that they will not disapprove, punish or restrict you?

Never   Sometimes   Often

8. Do your parents "use" what you tell them to find out if you are doing things they consider bad?

Never   Sometimes   Often

9. Do your parents criticize you for things you tell them about?

Never   Sometimes   Often

10. Do you feel that telling things to your parents will lead to an "inquisition" and put you on the spot?

Never   Sometimes   Often

11. Would you tell your parents more things about what you do or your life if they were less critical, more relaxed, or more understanding?

Never   Sometimes   Often

12. Would you like your parents to be more accepting of things you tell them?

Definitely   Probably   No

BEING TAKEN SERIOUSLY

13. Do your parents make you feel that the things that happen to you are not important or serious?

Never   Sometimes   Often

14. Do your parents make you feel that they do not have time to talk or listen to you?

Never   Sometimes   Often

15. Do your parents make you feel that they are willing to talk to you but not really listen to you and get your point-of-view?

Never   Sometimes   Often

16. Do your parents treat things you tell them lightly, saying things like "it's just a stage" or "you will grow out of it" or "it's something everybody goes through" or similar remarks?

Never   Sometimes   Often

17. Do your parents talk to you about serious personal things in life which affect them?

Never   Sometimes   Often

STANDARDS

18. Do your parents seem to have a different set of standards for you and for them?

Never   Sometimes   Often

19. Do your parents act as if they are perfect when in fact you know this is not true of them or anybody else?

Never   Sometimes   Often

20. Do your parents act as if most things have a good side and a bad side, with no in-between or differences of opinion?

Never   Sometimes   Often

21. Do your parents seem to be confused over what are ideal standards of behavior for you and what are reasonable or realistic for you?

Never   Sometimes   Often

22. Do your parents make you feel as if they could not accept you if they knew you were not perfect, and sometimes had weaknesses, failures, or made mistakes?

Never   Sometimes   Often

23. Do your parents make you feel as if they could not accept you if your standards did not agree with theirs, even though you have thought-out standards?

Never   Sometimes   Often

24. Add below any comments you feel will clarify your view of your communications with your parents.

THE GOOD KID BOOK

PACS SUMMARY

Based on the PACS ratings and your discussions of them, fill out this summary form in your own words. Spaces are left after each heading to fill in specific things which appeared to be problems. The "Other" section is for problems indicated from answers to item number 24, or for things which came up in discussion which do not fit any other heading. Use more or less space as you need it.

Area	*Problem?*
GENERAL COMMUNICATIONS	
1.	
2.	
CRITICALNESS	
1.	
2.	
3.	
4.	
BEING TAKES SERIOUSLY	
1.	
2.	
3.	
4.	
STANDARDS	
1.	
2.	
3.	
4.	
OTHER	
1.	
2.	

STORY CHECKLIST

Several categories of possible stories are given below. For each, think of something an individual your age might have done which you feel sure would upset your parents if they heard that you were the person. You may use real names, places, etc., if you want, but it is not necessary. For each category just jot down a brief note or two, sufficient to remind you of what your story idea is. You may make up more than one story for a category if you want to, or omit one if you feel you have no ideas for that category which would upset your parents.

1. Going someplace my parents disapprove of.

2. Being with someone or some kind of person who would upset my parents.

3. Doing something my parents would disapprove of or worry about.

4. Not doing something my parents feel I should do.

5. Talking with someone about something which would concern my parents.

6. Other—you think it up.

7. Other—you think it up.

IMPORTANT FAMILY MATTERS

1. Under "Topic" use some abbreviation so you will know what is referred to.

2. Under "Informed" mark a "Yes" if you have talked this over with the child in question and kept him or her up to date on what is going on. Otherwise mark a "No."

3. Under "Reason Not To" mark a "Yes" if there is some good reason not to tell your child or children about this topic, and a "No" if there is not. If you mark a "No" here and also mark a "No" under "Informed," circle the topic.

Topic	Informed	Reason Not To